# Praise for

# The Opposite of Certainty

"A beautiful sucker punch, like life. When the ground crumbles beneath your hopes, big dreams, and great expectations, what do you stand on and for? Where do you find the strength to keep going? You find it in this gem of a book."

—RON FOURNIER, *New York Times* BESTSELLING AUTHOR OF *LOVE THAT BOY*

"Somedays it's doughnuts and hot coffee. Other days it's gurneys and scans. That's true of almost every full life. Here's the good news: observant and warm, the writing of Janine Urbaniak Reid is the finest company on both kinds of days."

—KELLY CORRIGAN, *New York Times* BESTSELLING AUTHOR OF *TELL ME MORE* AND *THE MIDDLE PLACE*

"Full of spiritual grace and shining with a kind of rare hope, yes, it brings you to your knees but miraculously shows you that this might actually be the best vantage point to see the stars. Extraordinary."

—CAROLINE LEAVITT, *New York Times* BESTSELLING AUTHOR OF *PICTURES OF YOU* AND *CRUEL BEAUTIFUL WORLD*

# The Opposite of Certainty

*fear, faith, and life in between*

## Janine Urbaniak Reid

W PUBLISHING GROUP

AN IMPRINT OF THOMAS NELSON

Published in Nashville, Tennessee, by W Publishing Group, an imprint of Thomas Nelson.

Thomas Nelson titles may be purchased in bulk for educational, business, fundraising, or sales promotional use. For information, please e-mail SpecialMarkets@ThomasNelson.com.

Any Internet addresses, phone numbers, or company or product information printed in this book are offered as a resource and are not intended in any way to be or to imply an endorsement by Thomas Nelson, nor does Thomas Nelson vouch for the existence, content, or services of these sites, phone numbers, companies, or products beyond the life of this book.

**Library of Congress Cataloging-in-Publication Data**

Names: Reid, Janine Urbaniak, 1964- author.
Title: The opposite of certainty : fear, faith, and life in between / Janine Urbaniak Reid.
Description: Nashville : W Publishing an imprint of Thomas Nelson, 2020. | Includes bibliographical references. | Summary: "Janine Urbaniak Reid doesn't expect the chaos of an out-of-control life that begins when her young son's hand begins to shake. So she searches for a source of strength bigger than her circumstances, only to have her circumstances become even thornier with her own crisis. It is only then that Janine discovers hidden reserves of strength, humor, and a no-matter-what faith that looks nothing like she thought it would"—Provided by publisher.
Identifiers: LCCN 2019046945 (print) | LCCN 2019046946 (ebook) | ISBN 9780785230595 (paperback) | ISBN 9780785230618 (ebook)
Subjects: LCSH: Uncertainty. | Self-control. | Faith.
Classification: LCC BF463.U5 R45 2020 (print) | LCC BF463.U5 (ebook) | DDC 153.4—dc23
LC record available at https://lccn.loc.gov/2019046945
LC ebook record available at https://lccn.loc.gov/2019046946

*Printed in the United States of America*
20 21 22 23 24  LSC  10 9 8 7 6 5 4 3 2 1

*To Alan, Austin, Mason, and Sarah,*
*and to those who live in uncertainty*
*and those who are willing to sit in the*
*unknowing place alongside them*

*The opposite of faith is not doubt, but certainty.*
—ANNE LAMOTT

*Doubt is not the opposite of faith; it is one element of faith.*
—PAUL TILLICH

# Contents

# CONTENTS

# Foreword

## Anne Lamott

The Opposite of Certainty is the memoir of a woman who has managed to assemble a satisfying and safe life, with three children, a long marriage, a beautiful home surrounded by redwoods, several dogs, half a dozen (or so) cats, and a passion for spiritual understanding and union.

But they say that God comes to comfort the afflicted, and afflict the comfortable, and one day, her bright and charming young son's hands began to shake. This is the story of what happened next.

In this spiritual memoir, Janine Urbaniak Reid shares the deepest truths about life, beginning with how she kept it together (more or less) in the early days, and thereafter, through endless hospital stays while the family waited to learn whether Mason was even still inside his sleeping body. The journey takes her to the pits of despair, wild hope, and the day-to-day drama; but it also takes her deep into herself and the eternal questions we all ask ourselves. Who are we, really, way deep down, when everything we thought we knew turns out to have been conditional? Where do we land when the lifelong foundation from which we have lived seems to crumble beneath our feet? Where is faith in darkness and terror? Where can joy be found in uncertainty?

What is real and true, when what is going on can't actually be happening?

This is Janine's brilliant, rich, and breathtakingly honest and sometimes very funny account of defying the gravity of her circumstances. It is a book about life with a capital *L*. About a marriage, motherhood, the unfathomable salvation we find in friendships and nature. It is about grave doubt and faith—no-matter-what faith.

It's relatively easy to know who you are and what is true when things are going well and the details of your life are nicely in place, but as the old joke goes, "If you want to make God laugh, tell Her your plans." *The Opposite of Certainty* takes us from a perfectly planned and executed life, a secure and happy home, to the chaos of intensive care, from churches to brain institutes, bed (with her head under the pillow at three a.m.), and to a long, long and unlikely stay in the last place Janine ever expected to find peace—Texas.

It's the story of how a self-identified control freak learned to let go and let God (with whom she was barely speaking), and how she found the courage at her shakiest to do the deep dive into her precarious childhood, to find her authentic self and unearth new seeds of strength. This is a handbook for how we might all come through impossible times, transformed and yet more ourselves than we'd ever allowed ourselves to be. In these pages, the reader will find a strong and vulnerable new voice, a kindred soul, and bread for the journey.

# An Invitation

From one breath to the next, we exist in a place where there are no guarantees. We buttress against uncertainty and resist its gravitational pull. People like me try to control everything we possibly can to be safe. Sometimes, we're able to pretend that the ground underfoot is bedrock and the sky above predictable.

This book is for anyone who is tired of clenching against circumstance (or the news). It's not a how-to book or a how-not-to book. Oddly, in this story of my anything-but-predictable life, there is solace. Because there is good, and I often call it God, that illogically shows up in surprising forms, and in the most exhausting and terrifying moments, beauty can be revealed in the imperfect terrain.

My hope is to offer a companion in uncertain places, a place to identify in the heart of what's real and what matters.

# Nine Years Later

I want to tell this story as if it happened to someone else. I didn't want to find the black T-shirt. Mason only wore it two or three times. The shirt has a white cityscape graphic at the hem: silhouettes of the Golden Gate Bridge, the Transamerica Pyramid. It smells like thirteen-year-old Mason, only faintly now, under a dusty, unworn odor. I can't fold the shirt. I can't wash it or throw it away.

I'm not sure how it's still in my possession. Did the ER doctor at Marin General pass it along to the ambulance crew from Stanford? Did the ambulance crew leave it with us in the pediatric intensive care unit? I lost three pairs of prescription eyeglasses while Mason was hospitalized, but somehow, I never lost this shirt. Today I found it in a plastic bag, like a swimsuit sent home from summer camp.

I can't quite cry, and I can't put down the black shirt because the boy who put on this shirt that morning in December is gone. The boy whose life began when the ER doctor cut the shirt off his body is here in his place. That boy is cleaning his room now, so fully himself and so different at the same time—just like me.

This book reflects my remembering. It's the truth that woke me up at three a.m., the reality I felt and often resisted. I've related stories as I remember them, which means they are filtered through my perception and interpretation. If our brilliant doctors and nurses seem anything less than brilliant, that's on me. As for the medical professionals who weren't so brilliant, their names and identifying details have been changed in hopeful acknowledgment of their good intentions. These are people brave enough to try, even when the odds are against them, and that's something. I've also changed certain non-medical individuals' names and details to protect their privacy. My family and close friends have been kind enough to bless this telling, which says a lot about what strong and supportive people they are.

This is my story—messy, human parts included.

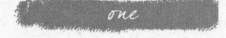

*one*

# Tremors

Mason and I are sitting on turquoise vinyl chairs in the waiting room of a pediatric neurologist at one of San Francisco's best hospitals. Mason is eight years old. We're both trying not to look at the other children in the other turquoise chairs. A few of them are bald, presumably from chemotherapy. Some have obvious developmental issues.

We don't fit here. Mason doesn't need chemotherapy. He has headaches, and his right hand shakes sometimes. He's a bit uncoordinated, but so am I. Things that come easily to his older brother are hard for Mason. He went through the entire Little League season without hitting a single pitch. Mason is like a Saint Bernard puppy, with big feet and hands that he hasn't grown into yet, which is cute, not worrisome.

I fill out a clipboard thick with forms. I don't know the answers to all the questions. How old was Mason when he first vocalized? Grasped a spoon? Sat unsupported? I suspect a more organized mother, even a mother of three, would have kept track of such things. Mason has been walking and vocalizing just fine for years now. I write "NORMAL" across the page.

Mason sees his pediatrician regularly and is thriving in every way. Still, I keep catching glimpses of a shadow, just beyond my line of sight. I've brought him to this neurologist so she can tell me that I'm overreacting. I want her to send me back to worrying about Mason's tooth brushing and broccoli intake. The normal worries of the normal mother of a normal eight-year-old boy.

We're here to see a pediatric neurologist whom I'll call Dr. Betsy Blake. She has shoulder-length blonde hair and a bare, unlined face that makes her look too young to be the person who is going to give us our pass and send us back to the pediatrician's office where the biggest worry is contracting a cold from a runny-nosed toddler. Still, it's a good hospital, one of the best. We're lucky to live close by.

"Boy, I wish I had eyelashes like those." She laughs as she checks the symmetry of Mason's pupils.

Mason smiles in his adorable one-dimpled way.

She winks at him, then listens to his heart, watches him touch his nose with his eyes closed, stand on one foot, and walk heel-toe along an imaginary straight line. It reminds me of the Presidential Fitness Test all the kids took when I was in fourth grade, but without the running and jumping. Within fifteen minutes, Dr. B. confirms what I've suspected for months: Mason has migraine headaches.

"If this were a debilitating problem, we'd recommend putting Mason on anti-depressants, which have been shown to inhibit chronic headaches in children," she says. "But these drugs can have side effects. A small percentage of normal children who take them become suicidal."

There's no way I'm going to give my happy boy a drug that might make him want to kill himself. Dr. B. and I agree on a better plan. I'll make sure he avoids headache triggers, like chocolate, dehydration, and getting too tired or too hungry.

As Mason and I gather ourselves to leave, I remember a small detail I'd forgotten to mention. "Sometimes Mason's hand shakes," I say.

The doctor gives Mason her pen.

"Write your name here." She supplies him a blank piece of paper.

The shaking is slight but noticeable as Mason presses through and forms letters on the page.

"It's a normal tremor," Dr. B. says. "Some people just shake a little."

I inhale deeply for the first time since we got here. I knew it. I was just being a hypervigilant mom. Mason is normal. Better than normal. This doctor is smart, intuitive even. It'll be a challenge to keep him away from chocolate, but we'll manage.

# two

# Chocolate Eggs and Women in Barbie Doll Blouses

We're having a weekend family vacation at a hotel where the pool is heated and draped in dense purple bougainvillea. Best of all, there's an Easter-egg hunt organized by someone other than me.

I feel guilty not spending Easter morning in church. I don't want my children to grow up thinking Easter is just about jelly beans and stuffed bunnies. But the hotel garden is lush with azaleas and a lawn that seems to have been manicured with tiny scissors. The kids are nearly jumping out of their dress-up shoes waiting for the hunt to begin.

When the Easter Bunny gives the go-ahead, Mason takes off with the kind of concentration I hope he'll bring to the SATs someday. Eleven-year-old Austin quickly fills his basket, then helps six-year-old Sarah fill hers. Alan puts his arm around me to warm against the chilly ocean breeze.

Going away for Easter freed us from having to choose between spending the holiday with my mom and her husband, Art, or with my dad and his fiancée, Cecelia. Alan's parents live on the East Coast, so they aren't contenders for the more routine holiday appearances.

Alan and I both have parents who divorced after more than twenty years of marriage. We haven't inherited the manual for married bliss, but usually we're a smooth-running machine. The past two years have been different. Difficult. I'm sure it's because we have so little time together. Alan travels for work at least four days a week, so I'm in charge at home. There's the problem of reentry.

At home, I know how things are supposed to be. What I don't know I make up, and the kids don't seem to notice. I try to remember that I have an equal partner in this. Mostly I try to educate Alan, to bring him along to the "right" way of doing things, whether it's choosing a school for the kids or loading the dishwasher. Letting go is not my strength; neither is compromise. I might've learned this from my mother, the most capable person I know, who is also always right.

I feel a pang of missing my mom. She's probably roasting Polish sausage for Easter brunch. I'll call later and try not to hear the catch of disappointment in her voice over the missed holiday.

Sitting at a pretty table overlooking a lush garden, I sip my black tea from a paper cup softened by too many refills at the coffee station the hotel has set up for tired parents. The idea of three nights away was more relaxing than the reality of five of us in one hotel room.

I lean into Alan, and he kisses the top of my head. I remind myself that this trip is about starting our own family traditions. Alan has left his phone in the hotel room. I squeeze his hand, a bit of positive affirmation for his efforts to stay present with the kids and me.

I've been trying to be a better wife. Someone who isn't constantly distracted by her children. Someone who doesn't surrender to the exhaustion that goes with those children. My husband has become a big man in the world, attracting the attention of a lot of people, including women who are not me. My friend Joan says, "Of course you want other women to think your husband is fabulous." But I didn't marry George Clooney. If I had, I would have expected this.

I married a guy who laughed too loud at the movies, sometimes at the wrong parts. I married a guy who didn't flirt.

---

I knew Alan through a friend. At the time, I'd been taking a break from dating after some miscalculations. I'd arrived at the point in my young life where I appreciated nights alone in my studio apartment with Humphrey Bogart and Lauren Bacall movies.

I was twenty-five when we first connected at a benefit dance party in Golden Gate Park's Hall of Flowers. I paid my ten dollars at the door and stood by myself, pretending not to feel awkward. That's when Alan appeared and asked me to dance.

The Beatles' song "I Saw Her Standing There" was playing, which was out of the ordinary because this was more of a Cure kind of crowd. Alan danced with zero self-consciousness, hopping on one leg, then the other in an I-could-be-dancing-outside-in-a-park-barefoot kind of approach. He might look conservative in his white button-down shirt, but he clearly had been to a Grateful Dead show or a hundred of them. He smiled and absently smoothed his short, curly hair. The next song cued up and we kept dancing. I noticed the broad sweep of his cheekbones, which wasn't immediately obvious under his round, wire-rimmed glasses.

"Do you want a bottle of water?" he asked when the music switched to something more predictable by Flock of Seagulls.

I didn't know that he spent his last dollar on that bottle of water, but while I drank it he told me he'd gone back to college and recently graduated. In addition to his Financial District internship, he'd spent last weekend selling long-distance telephone service at the Chinatown

Street Fair. He had potential, along with kind eyes and an easy laugh. He also didn't drink, and neither did I.

We danced to a few more songs. The party wound down.

"Are you going to coffee?" he asked.

"No." I paused waiting for the invitation.

"Okay," he said. He hadn't even gotten my phone number.

I went home to my VCR.

We didn't see each other until three weeks later when Alan "co-incidentally" appeared at a laundromat in my neighborhood. He left his unwashed clothes with his roommate, and we went to a movie. I found myself distracted. My attention was drawn to Alan. I glanced at him; he was looking at me too. I smiled, a little embarrassed. He offered me popcorn.

"You couldn't keep your eyes off me," he said much later.

"Oh, no," I said. "Every time I looked you were staring at me."

I drove him home and said goodbye with a chaste but promising kiss. He waved from the door of the tired Victorian where he lived with three roommates in a part of the city that would quadruple in value once the freeway dissecting it was torn down years later. But that night I locked my car doors and didn't linger at stop signs. I found myself smiling as I accelerated onto Van Ness, and I said out loud to no one, "I'm going to marry that guy."

A few months later I dropped him off at the corner of Post and Montgomery before the six a.m. West Coast stock market start time; the internship had turned into a job. He wore a gray Brooks Brothers suit he'd found at a Pacific Heights thrift shop, which I'd affection-ately dubbed his "dead banker's suit." He looked good, tall and nicely proportioned, striped tie knotted just right. He leaned over to kiss me goodbye.

"I love you," he said for the first time.

"Thank you," I mumbled.

I suspected I loved him, but this was too important for a knee-jerk

"I love you too." That's how I knew: the fluttery delight I felt inside when I heard his voice on the phone or noticed his silhouette in a doorway; the way we didn't have to think of things to say because words just flowed. We both believed in a God that we couldn't pin down or define, a reliable, loving presence that would give us the strength and direction we needed when we needed it. Most important, he laughed at my jokes; he got them; he got me. He didn't complain that I worked too much. He loved that I had a career, and that I was good at it. I knew he'd do well. There wasn't any doubt. He also didn't flirt with waitresses or check out women jogging by. He wasn't that guy.

"I love you," I said while we shared a pepperoni pizza in my studio apartment a few nights later. The sunset was reflecting off Russian Hill, casting a pretty melon color on the white walls, a crayon shade I'd used many times as a girl to draw princess gowns and fairy godmothers.

We married three years later in a small, heartfelt ceremony in a stone church on the Marin side of San Francisco Bay. I hired the only guitar-playing singer in the Bay Area who didn't know the Grateful Dead's "Uncle John's Band." But I gave her a cassette so she could learn it, and I could surprise Alan. I overheard a friend comment at our reception, "He adores her." It was wonderful to be adored, but that wasn't the point. I could count on Alan, and he could count on me. This was our creed, unspoken but unwavering.

So it startled me when the boyfriend flush with potential—now father of my three children—came home a few months ago shaken, surprised, and told me that a woman tried to kiss him. A woman I knew and now loathed. Alan assured me he wasn't interested. If he had been, he pointed out, he wouldn't have told me. Still, I was disturbed.

I repeated the story to a friend, who said, "Whose husband hasn't been kissed by some tramp?" I guess I'm naïve. My mom put aside some of her own complicated experiences to teach me that women should look out for each other. I wanted to believe that other women honor the code, that there is a code.

I told my friend that the woman who'd tried to kiss my husband was younger and that the last time I'd seen her, her ampleness had spilled out of her tiny Barbie doll blouse. It was the kind of exposure that once caused my nursing toddler to point at a similarly endowed woman and yell, "Milk!"

"I know a great plastic surgeon," my soon-to-be-former friend said, eyeing my chest. "Friends of mine have done it to spice things up. Feel good about themselves."

I crossed my arms. Implants weren't the answer. It just wasn't me. What I needed was something that couldn't be bought or surgically improved.

The problem: as Alan's world keeps getting bigger, I've started losing my footing in my own. I'm somebody's wife, several somebodies' mother, but who exactly am I again?

I used to be a young vice president of a small-but-mighty public relations agency. I had a business card and an expensive leather briefcase to prove it. But now, as my kids thrive and my husband earns his elite frequent flyer status, I'm asked to make soup for kindergarten open houses. I love my life, really. It's just that sometimes I can't feel myself in my skin.

As a hedge against insanity, I signed up for a series of upcoming writing retreats, hoping to find myself on the pages of the fresh, untouched composition books now languishing in my suitcase.

---

I drain another cup of tea. Austin points to a pink plastic egg hidden under a hedge and nudges Sarah to go for it. Mason's lips have taken on the purple tinge of a handful of jelly beans. I love these kids. I really do.

After the egg hunt, the five of us head for the hotel restaurant for brunch. The waitress fills our glasses with fresh-squeezed orange juice—liquid gold at six dollars a glass. "Finish your juice," I tell Mason. Since Dr. B. named dehydration as a headache trigger, I've been reminding Mason to drink at least ten times a day, but keeping track of his liquid intake has been extra challenging on vacation. And from the look of his white shirt, it also appears that he's indulged in contraband chocolate eggs, though he's not complaining about a headache, not right now.

Mason lifts his glass. His right hand shakes wildly, and he can't seem to get the glass to his mouth. His hand jerks in front of his face. I'm about to tell him to knock it off because this must be a bad joke. Then I realize he can't control it when he reaches out with his left hand to steady the right. The juice pours down the front of his polo shirt, all over his chair and onto the floor.

"I'm sorry," he says, his eyes filled with tears.

Alan and I dry him off with napkins, pretending we aren't worried. I make sure Mason finishes his omelet and two glasses of water. His shaking subsides.

Now shaking myself, I take my phone into the hallway outside the restaurant and leave an urgent message for Dr. B.

*three*

# What's Wrong with This Picture?

I don't want to be back in the hospital neurology department. I don't want to believe that something is really wrong with my son. But here we are.

"Can you walk a straight line for me, Mason?" Dr. B. asks gently.

Mason performs an exaggerated version of a drunk stumble, then straightens up and looks from Dr. B. to me, waiting for our reaction. The doctor laughs. I manage a smile to show that I'm a supportive mom, but I really want to tell him to knock it off so we can get to the part where Dr. B. tells me he's okay. As if he's read my mind, he finishes his assignment with the grace and precision of a tightrope walker.

Dr. B. asks Mason to hold out his hands. They're shaking more than they were last month, even last week.

"You have beautiful green eyes," the doctor tells my son. Then she turns to me.

"Mason has a 'normal' tremor, as we discussed last time," she says. "I'm guessing that the Easter spill happened because his blood sugar was too low."

I don't immediately remember that his blood sugar was likely high on jelly beans. We did have a late breakfast that day. The doctor turns her gaze to Mason. "Mason, you need to make sure you have something to eat and drink first thing after you wake up every morning. Okay? Will you do that for me?"

"Okay," Mason says, a little glumly.

---

Years ago we rescued a dog who is a lot like me. Jesse flinches at the oddest sounds—a bird in the garden, a car door slamming in the driveway. I speak to him in a tender voice, but he still twitches and worries. I do too. But I learn to live with it, like someone with an overdeveloped sense of smell. I joke that I use my powers for good now, and that includes my complete focus on giving my kids a happy life, which means they won't ever be hurt, scared, or scarred.

The first morning I left baby Austin to go back to work, I cried off my mascara before I got to the Golden Gate Bridge. In the months that followed, I showed up minimally late, and left exactly on time with my sad, not-even-half-filled pumped bottles of breast milk. One night I was headed out the door when my boss waved me into the conference room where the rest of the team was assembled with pens poised over notepads. I wore my coat with my purse and discreet insulated bag slung over my shoulder. We'd been working on a new business proposal for a big-name corporation.

"This is really important," my boss explained. "If you're not stressed out about it, you don't care." She didn't look at me directly, but she didn't need to. All I could think about was the traffic backing up between me and my baby.

I lasted a little while longer at that job. Alan was carrying his suitcase up the front steps when I explained that I had a proposal of my own. I waited for him to take off his jacket and settle into a plate of leftover spaghetti before I handed him my spreadsheet.

"This is what it costs for me to work," I said. I'd added up the bridge tolls, parking, the babysitter, the dry cleaning, the panty hose (it was 1995), and take-out food. In the next column, I listed my paltry salary.

"Okay," he said, balancing six-month-old Austin on his lap.

I give birth to two more children while assembling my life brick by brick, like the third little pig; no wolves would hurt my children, no big winds. I'm not sure when the noun *parent* morphed into a verb, but it becomes my singular dedication, taking care of these little people, helping them reach their potential, giving them so much love and protection that they'll never develop an empty space inside—the one my sober friends refer to as "the God-shaped hole."

Before I was old enough to name it, I became aware of the porousness of this human life, the missing something, that enduring riddle of a separateness on this side of the sky. I assumed that the unnamed emptiness was unique to me—a personal flaw—because nobody talked about it. Growing up, I saw family members try to fill it as best they could. Some, like my dad and my grandpa, drank too much. Others ate too much or too little. There were people like my mom, who ironed the drinkers' shirts and bleached their whites so that no one would notice. And then there were the predators who reached for girls like me, whose parents were distracted trying to remedy their own dis-ease. Yes, we went to church most Sundays, even confession on Saturdays, but we only admitted those sins that wouldn't make us look too bad in the eyes of the priest and the Almighty.

I learned to approach the world like one of those what's-wrong-with-this-picture puzzles in *Highlights* magazine, where you circle things like a fork drawn into the leaves of a tree or a hippo inside a car. I anticipated trouble so that I could outsmart it. I tally this as a benefit of my upbringing, not dwelling on the downside, which is the overcaffeinated newsreel of what-might-go-bad that still runs behind my eyelids too many nights.

I don't want my children to ever feel the way I did, to experience that kind of hurt, fear, and self-doubt. So any philosophy that promises to protect and nurture has my attention. I can't control everything in my children's lives, but I build fortifications where I can.

By this time, the kids attend an idyllic little school in the idyllic village of Mill Valley a few miles south of us. It's perfect. The former parochial school has been painstakingly restored by a group of parents dedicated to bringing their children an education that will nourish their souls as well as their minds, ultimately landing them in prestigious universities or fashionable liberal arts colleges, while ensuring a lifelong passion for organic gardening and environmental activism.

The school's hallways are decorated with watercolors the children painted. The floors, fixtures, and old oak banisters glow with the effortless antique sheen on display at the pricey shops down the street. Every aspect of the school experience has been thought through. The classroom windows are draped with gauzy curtains in soft pastel shades that correspond to the children's developmental stages: pink for kindergarten, yellow for first grade, and so forth.

The children take a knitting class three times a week. They create woolen gnomes and pencil cases while knitting strong connections in their brains, as scientifically proven by someone somewhere in Europe.

Mason loves school. Knitting is hard for him because of his tremor, but he loves history class and excels in the math games. He gets along well with his classmates—except for the boy who pummeled him in the back seat while another mother drove them to a birthday party. This resulted in laborious processing and endless discussions with several well-intentioned teachers who were reluctant to burden the pummeler with any sort of negative diagnosis. The drama was short-lived, the pummeler moved to a different school, and peace prevailed.

Mason is friends with everyone, and he does what's expected of him. So I'm not concerned when his fourth-grade teacher, Dirk, asks me to meet with him after school.

Dirk sits in one of the children's chairs and motions for me to join him.

"Mason is having trouble keeping up with the written work," says Dirk, smoothing his shaved head absently. "He can think faster than he can write. The tremor is starting to hold him back."

I'm not sure what to say. I've already explained the normal tremor to Dirk, warned him about Mason's blood sugar, hydration (which turns out to be a headache trigger), and avoiding gluten. None of that, apparently, is enough.

"I have a referral for you: a chiropractic neurologist in San Francisco," Dirk says.

I've never heard of that specialty, but I like the idea of doing something. My spine relaxes at the thought. I thank Dirk for the recommendation. That afternoon I call and make an appointment.

*four*

# On My Knees

Mason is lying on his back on the paper-covered exam table, arms crossed under his head, the soles of his Nikes worn through from Razor-scootering down our driveway. I don't usually get this view of his shoes. I hope Dr. Azzolino doesn't think I'm a careless mother.

"So when did Mason's tremor start?" Dr. Azzolino is tall, in his mid-thirties, with a profile suitable for a Roman coin. He wears a white shirt and a shiny silk tie.

"I first noticed it two years ago," I answer. "I took him to a neurologist who said it was a 'normal' tremor. But it's getting worse . . ."

As I speak, Dr. Azzolino types into his laptop.

"Okay, Mason," he says. "Time to sit up."

Mason springs into a seated position.

"Can you close your eyes and touch your nose?"

Mason closes his eyes and points to his forehead, quickly peeking to gauge the doctor's reaction.

Dr. Azzolino laughs, and so does Mason.

After the routine neuro exam, Dr. Azzolino straps goggles on

Mason. They record his eye movements on a screen while the doctor stimulates certain parts of Mason's brain with light and movement.

At the end of the exam, Mason goes to the bathroom, and Dr. Azzolino leans in close to me.

"There's something going on in his cerebellum," Dr. Azzolino says. "He needs an MRI."

My throat clenches. It's difficult to draw a breath, harder to think.

"But . . . but . . . the pediatric neurologist said it's just migraine headaches," I stammer. "She didn't mention an MRI."

I don't like opening a door to something potentially being wrong, as if by the simple fact of the door being open some sharp-beaked tragedy might fly in and lay eggs. I know this isn't logical. I think of all the prenatal tests I had over three pregnancies. The worst part was waiting to be told everything was fine—that all my anxieties and future-tripping were for nothing.

"Why not take a picture?" Dr. Azzolino asks softly. "Just to make sure everything's okay."

There is only one reason not to get an MRI: I'm afraid. Normal kids don't get pictures of their brains, and I want my son to be normal, at least in the way that means he's healthy. I call the local imaging center anyway and schedule the scan.

Two days later, Mason is encapsulated in a scanner, the machine clicking and humming around him. "Can I get a picture to take back to school with me?" Mason asks. "I want to show everyone my brain."

"I'll see what I can do," a technician named Larry says, then retreats behind the door of his glass-walled control booth.

I sit in a chair beside the scanner with a reassuring hand on Mason's ankle, the only part of him I can reach. The machine is loud through the yellow foam earplugs the technician gave me. It's like being on a runway with jets taking off and landing, if those jets also made random clicking sounds.

The scan takes forty-five minutes. We're waiting in the reception area when Larry comes out with a twelve-by-twelve-inch sheet of film and hands it to Mason, who holds the square to the overhead fluorescent light. It looks like the ultrasounds I'd seen of my babies before the technology got photographic. There are vague shapes in shades of gray. I can make out Mason's eye sockets, his teeth, including the ones that haven't come in yet, and in a vague, scribbled kind of way, his brain. Nothing out of the ordinary there. Hundreds of deeper and more detailed pictures of Mason's brain will be reviewed by a radiologist, who will have a report to us in about a week. But, surely, I'd see anything scary if it was there.

I tell myself I've been silly to worry. The untethered fear has been the worst part. Now I can cross "MRI" off my to-do list.

*five*

# Boze Grozi

**B**oze Grozi roughly translated means "What did you do to make God so mad at you?" It was a curse and a warning my Polish grandmothers spoke in the face of tragedy, stupidity, or dumb luck. God kept score. My grandmothers tentatively trusted the hippie son of a thunderbolt-wielding God, but they reflexively ducked when it started to rain. My good-intentioned parents tried to outrun this kind of thinking (and my father's alcoholism) by moving across the country. When we arrived in Los Angeles from our native Chicago, they traded their Old Testament upbringing for guitar mass on Saturday evenings. They read *Jonathan Livingston Seagull* and bought *Godspell* on eight-track. They were too smart for *Boze Grozi*. Me? I grew up to check all the boxes put before me: college degree, career requiring a dry-clean-only wardrobe, no unplanned pregnancies or premature marriages. When it became clear I'd drawn the genetic short straw with alcoholism, I got sober fast and young, which was more blessing than curse. I was too smart for this *Boze Grozi* (and lucky so far). But it turns out, the paradigm lives in me like a dormant virus. If I want to keep my family safe, it's simple: I just have to do everything right.

Alan and I settled in a safe and nonpolluted neighborhood in Marin County, California. Our house was the vision of a San Francisco baker (sourdough bread and butter cookies) and WWI veteran who transplanted his family into this sleepy mission town the same year the Golden Gate Bridge opened. The land around us is still wild, shaded by redwoods, bay trees, and manzanita. Poison oak and wild blackberry push their way through English ivy.

Alan hung a rope swing from a limb of one of the aged oaks. We throw birthday parties for our kids in the redwood grove behind the house, where decades ago someone built two long tables out of logs and boards. I like the patina of the place, the touch of the people who were here before. Our children live among the trees, and I can walk to a coffee shop.

I am ridiculously blessed, and I do believe in the benevolent God who was introduced to me when I stopped drinking. I was only twenty-four when one hangover morning the words came out of my mouth, "You're an alcoholic." By then my dad was sober. I'd started therapy. I admitted that I could become an alcoholic someday—when I was really, really old—if I didn't watch it.

I tried not to drink very often. I could manage this for weeks, maybe even a month or so. Then came a random Saturday morning and a date with nobody especially important.

"Do you want to share a beer?" the guy asked.

"Sure," I answered because I'm a polite person. How could sharing a beer at eleven a.m. hurt anyone? But half a beer morphed into margaritas, then many dreamy, foggy glasses of red wine and white, too, because I think I ate fish.

I was lucky. By this time, I hadn't destroyed much besides my self-esteem, which had never been a real strength anyway. I felt like there was something deep down wrong with me, that the true me was best kept hidden away. That first day sober was like putting on prescription glasses for the first time.

*I don't want to have to drink again. I don't want to die.* This mantra repeated in my head. It didn't seem possible I possessed the gene that propelled my grandfather into alcohol-withdrawal seizures after surgery for bladder cancer. I was a *nice* girl. I had graduated early from college. I ran two miles almost every day. I had a job, a résumé. One achievement at a time, I'd reinforced a sea wall against what I feared lived inside me. But my childhood cast stubborn shadows. Life still looked a lot like one of those what's-wrong-with-this-picture puzzles, only now I worried that someone might spot me in a tree with a fork. Survival meant not letting anyone know what was wrong with me, especially not making mistakes. So it didn't make sense that I'd abdicate control of my mind, body, and spirit to a liquid that could be poured and swallowed. But how could I not?

I started at a new high school when my family moved from Southern to Northern California in 1978, and for the first time ever I wasn't among the last girls picked for a soccer team during PE. The guy picking the teams didn't care that I couldn't kick the ball and run at the same time. They didn't know I was *that* girl. I didn't recognize myself when I looked in the mirror, thick glasses replaced by contact lenses, no more buck teeth, braces, or headgear, instead a slightly pleading but straight-toothed smile.

The outsides were coming along, so it was more important than ever that I keep the inside stuff buried somewhere soundproof. It was difficult knowing what to say to people, trying so hard to reveal so little. Most of all, it was exhausting trying to be so good and never make mistakes. When I got drunk for the first time, I felt free. I thought, *I wish I could feel this way all the time.* I was hilariously funny,

THE OPPOSITE OF CERTAINTY

shockingly pretty, and a surprisingly good dancer. There are snapshot memories of being pushed into a shower wearing jeans and a bra. I woke up vomiting, knees skinned, minus a contact lens. I couldn't wait to do it again.

For the next nine years, I drunkenly navigated the line between fun and humiliation with varying success. Some nights were unmemorable. Some I wish I could forget. Still others are completely blank, like my brain compassionately neglected to hit the record button. I might not have put the time in drinking that my dad or grandfather had, but for me it was enough.

Those first weeks sober, the nightmares were the worst. I woke up alone in my apartment consumed by the crushing terror of five-year-old me, who had been preyed on all those years ago by a man in my mother's family. I had never told anyone. I called my friend Marion. She didn't drink, and she wasn't afraid all the time either.

"You're not hiding from it anymore, so now you can heal," she said.

"But I feel like I'm going to crawl out of my skin."

"It's like frostbite. You're thawing out and that hurts," she explained. "It gets better."

The other worst part was admitting defeat when my survival depended on having a plan, being right and avoiding danger/humiliation/death. "Being right" was another bright shiny object I used to distract from the fear that threatened to eat me from the inside out. Now I was pitiful. I sobbed because I'd rather be anything else.

My family had sought out its first therapist when I was ten. There was some family problem I can't remember, but it certainly wasn't Dad's drinking because we didn't talk about that. On the way home, Mom promised to stop at the library so I could check out five pounds of hardcover books above my reading level.

The therapist, who I'll call Mr. McVee, met with each family member separately. I spent my hour telling him how much I liked my teacher, how I planned to be a lawyer (by now Mom was a legal secretary), and how I liked reading and cats. I remembered my fourth-grade teacher's expression when I shared too much during circle time. I didn't want Mr. McVee to look at me the same way, so I smiled until my face ached through my braces and headgear.

"You don't have anything to worry about with that one," Mr. McVee assured my parents. As they suspected, I was on the right track.

This is one reason why I never told anyone my full story: I couldn't stand the wilt in their eyes that acknowledged the hurt I pretended wasn't there. Another worst part of hitting this bottom was admitting I didn't know how to do life. I thought success/contentment/happiness were within reach, though most often too slippery to hold on to. All I had to do was say the right thing, make my straight hair curl, get promoted, fit into my jeans, find the right boyfriend, and go to church once in a while to remind God of my good intentions. I'd always had a plan. Now my thinking had failed me. This created just enough of an opening for a spirit that didn't come in a bottle.

Sober friends talked about not being able to control their drinking and the humiliation I knew but didn't dare speak aloud. Many had carried secrets like mine. It's in this "we" that I found a connection to a Source bigger than my problem. This new and possibly trustworthy version of God presented me with friends who held me even when I told the truth, especially then. It was a "come as you are" faith that got me through the days when my skin felt ill-fitting and my mind replayed its biggest anxieties like a torturous Looney Tunes loop.

I slowly gained confidence that this God thing wasn't just a method of control honed by Polish grandmothers. I did all the things that people do to stay sober, relieved that there was a plan. I prayed. I helped others. I made up for harms done. I did good things, and good things happened in my life. I checked boxes, and the formula worked.

Then I had children.

I had been sober for six years when Alan held my hand as the epidural took hold after nineteen valiant hours of unmedicated labor. Contractions had stalled, and the obstetrician encouraged us to rest. I'd hired a doula named Esther to support us in having a peaceful, intervention-free birth that would virtually guarantee a healthy, well-adjusted baby.

When walking, squatting, and crying didn't make the strong contractions come back, Esther asked, "Why do you think your baby doesn't want to come?" I sobbed and threw up. Esther looked satisfied, like she'd struck a chord. Really, it was terror I felt, not truth. I was trying so hard, and I couldn't make this baby come in my reasonable, not-scary, less painful timeframe. I'd been talking to him, holding hands on my expanding belly for nine months. Alan and I loved him without question or condition.

I prayed, "Help." I promised my baby, "It's going to be a great life." Austin arrived early the next morning—on his time, not mine.

This experience of powerlessness, though profound, was easily overshadowed by the protective instinct that flooded me, a certainty that if a mountain lion wandered into the yard, it would turn and run at the sight of me. Predators of any species didn't stand a chance. I'd done therapy. When a certain teenage boy down the street offered to babysit, I thanked him, but inside I screamed, "Hell no!"

Hypervigilance would be the gift of my upbringing. When I returned to work, the sitter, a thirty-five-year-old mother of two, was thoroughly vetted. I gathered up the childhood hurt along with my good-girl desperation and macraméd them into a kind of superhero coil, something golden that Wonder Woman might clip to her belt. The feeling only grew with the births of Mason and Sarah. No one would hurt my children.

Our house is secured to its foundation with six-inch steel bolts, the stone chimney reinforced, and the water heater strapped to studs in the wall. I fill our storage room with bottled water, protein bars, and D batteries. I keep a close eye on the strange man who naps in his car at the end of our block. I watch for sleeper waves at the beach, and sociopaths posing as magazine salesmen. It's exhausting, but it's my duty as a mother, a good mother, to anticipate danger and avoid it.

I pray most days, asking to be useful to my family and in the world. I pray that the people I love be protected and safe. I believe in God; I just don't always trust Him alone with my kids.

# six

# Inside Out

We expect the results from Mason's MRI in a few days. There's plenty to distract me in the meantime. I clean the dashboard of the minivan with the baby wipes, waiting for Sarah and Mason to get out of school. I gather fruit leather wrappers and deflated juice boxes into an empty paper bag. No doubt it will be a mess by the end of the day, but the momentary absence of trash gives me the illusion of order in my life.

My phone rings. It's Alan.

"You need to bring Mason to Dr. Azzolino's office. There's something on the MRI."

I hear his words, but they make no sense. "What do you mean?"

I have rarely heard fear in Alan's voice, so I don't recognize it at first.

"I just got off the phone with them," Alan's voice shakes. "I'll meet you there."

I feel as if I've been hit by the yellow school bus though it's still parked at the curb. I exit my body. I hover above, watching myself open the van door and stand on wobbly legs. My ears ring with the children's voices, their laughter. I've been launched outside this happy reality where children race out school doors burdened only by their brightly colored backpacks. I'm untethered. I watch myself ask the father of a boy from Sarah's class if he can take her home with them. Then I call a friend whose son is in Austin's class and ask her to pick him up. I'm waiting for Mason as he walks down the steps of the school.

"We need to go back to Dr. Azzolino's," I say, invoking a calm I don't feel.

The possibility of something awful has not cracked into Mason's consciousness yet. It's barely cracked mine. He gets in the van, belts up, and stares out the window. He's tired, more tired than usual, but he's had another good day at school, and tomorrow his class is going on a field trip.

I hand him a fruit leather and turn on the *Shrek* soundtrack. I hope the familiar songs will give him the reassurance I can't muster. We pass the Sausalito exit and enter the rainbow tunnel. Nothing is remarkable. Nothing has changed. I keep my focus on the white lines on the black road as we near the Golden Gate.

*Now that we know what's wrong, we can fix it. We'll find a good doctor who will make the tremors and the headaches go away.* I repeat this thought to myself like a mantra. I refuse to let the scarier possibilities in. Doctors can do remarkable things with the brain; things that would have been impossible just a few years ago. We'll track down the right specialist. Our insurance is intact. Alan is smart, and so am I. We'll figure it out.

I notice that the sky is an incongruous color of blue. A pickup truck cuts in front of me at the toll plaza, and I scream, "Bastard!"

"Mom!" Mason sounds worried.

Alan waits for us in front of Dr. Azzolino's office, dressed in a gray suit. He puts his arm around Mason and speaks in a cheerful voice. His eyes are frantic.

We're fifteen minutes early, so the three of us walk a block to Peet's Coffee. My throat is so dry it's difficult to talk. I buy Mason a vanilla milk and order a chamomile tea, something I never drink before ten p.m.

Dr. Azzolino asks Mason to wait with the receptionist while Alan and I follow him into a small exam room. He keeps his face expressionless, his voice even, but I can tell he is upset. He has kids too, he tells us.

"There's a tumor in Mason's brain."

My hot tea splatters on the carpet and the wall. I try to mop it up with the sleeve of my sweater, but Dr. Azzolino puts his hand on mine. "Leave it."

"Mason needs to see a pediatric neurosurgeon right away," he continues.

I'm not sure any of this can be true, but I know that it is.

Alan tucks the disk with Mason's MRI on it into the pocket of his suit jacket.

We must get the tumor out of Mason *now*. I know we're both thinking the same thought. You don't drive home and have dinner after receiving news like this. You *do* something.

Alan and Dr. Azzolino leave polite but urgent voice-mail messages for several pediatric neurosurgeons. No one is available at four thirty on a Thursday afternoon. We can't bring Mason to the emergency room because there's no bleeding to stop, no poison to purge. He is the same boy who was playing dodgeball just a few hours ago, who is flipping through a surfing magazine in Dr. Azzolino's waiting room wondering what's taking us so long.

If I wasn't distracted by the sound of my heartbeat echoing inside of my head and my inability to breathe, I might remember that Mason has had headaches and tremors for years. But hearing the words *brain* and *tumor* in the same sentence as my son's name leaves no room for perspective.

Alan remembers an old roommate whose brother is a neurosurgeon at a nearby hospital. Dr. Weber agrees to see us right away. We race up Pacific Street with Mason in the back seat.

"We're going to see a special brain doctor," I say.

A few moments later, as Alan and I whisper, frantically trying to figure out what to do, one or the other of us says the word *tumor*.

Mason's head appears between the front seats.

"Do I have a brain tumor?" he asks, his stunned voice almost adult.

This is not the right way to tell a kid he has a tumor. I should be in the back seat, holding him, explaining in a way that will not scare him. It is all horribly wrong, like we've switched movies halfway through. I'm lost. I reach between the seats and hold Mason's hand, his fingers sticky and warm.

"I'm so sorry, honey." I wipe my tears with the back of my sleeve. "Now at least we know what's causing your headaches and your tremor. We can find a doctor to fix it."

Mason sits back. His eyes in the rearview mirror are big, round, and scared. The rest of the ride is silent.

Alan gives Dr. Weber the MRI disk. The doctor projects the images onto a computer screen so we can all see them. He speaks in a normal voice, as if he isn't afraid. He points to a shadowy mass the size of a lemon. Tears flow out of me now, rivers of them. I want to stop crying, but I can't.

"Mason has probably had the tumor his entire life," Dr. Weber says. "If a person were to grow a tumor like this quickly, he would be noticeably sick, which Mason clearly is not."

The neurosurgeon looks from Alan, to Mason, to me. "Do you understand what I'm saying? This looks like a slow-growing tumor. You have time to figure out what to do."

The next morning we're back in the depressing gray medical building. A friend of a friend who's on the hospital board of directors finagled us an appointment with a neuro-oncologist whom I'll call Dr. Alba. It's his job to tell us how to get rid of the tumor. Every second we don't know the answer is unbearable.

My head throbs from crying all night, and I have an out-of-body feeling, as if my hands can't quite grip the steering wheel of myself. My anger about Dr. B.'s two-year misdiagnosis is pulsing through me like molten lava. It burns, but it's keeping me upright and giving me the clarity to form thoughts.

"The chiropractic neurologist ordered a scan," I say. "And there it was. A tumor in his brain." The words rush out of my mouth. The doctor recoils reflexively at the word chiropractic. "I'd taken him to Dr. B. for two years for the headaches and the tremor. She never once mentioned an MRI."

"I've reviewed Mason's records," Dr. Alba says. "There's no way Dr. B. could have known he had a tumor."

Dr. Alba sounds to me as if he's reading from a hospital legal brief. I manage to keep my anger in my mouth and my mouth shut, in case the kids of nice parents get better treatment. Then he rifles through a manila folder with Mason's name on the tab.

"It says here that Dr. B. ordered a blood test for Mason back in April, and you didn't follow up on that until last month?"

No blood test would have shown the tumor, still, his blow lands in my chest with a thud. It seems the hot potato of blame trumps whatever VIP status we might have as friends of friends of a hospital board member. Now I'm sweating guilt along with anger.

"The chiropractic neurologist knew something was wrong in Mason's cerebellum within an hour of meeting him," I snap. "The only difference between what he did and what Dr. B. did was that he ordered a scan."

Alan and I exchange a look. As expected, the hospital is fortifying its defenses. I don't want to sue anybody. I just want someone to cure my son.

Alan puts his cold, damp hand on top of mine. "What can you tell us after seeing the scan?" he asks, before I alienate the doctor who can tell us how to fix this. Mason sits hunched over on the exam table, chewing on his thumbnail, his face blank. He looks younger than ten and more vulnerable than I've ever seen him. I'm already missing the confident boy who challenges the other kids to ball games on the playground, who laughs easily and often.

"You need to see a neurosurgeon who can remove the tumor," Dr. Alba says. "We'll talk about next steps—radiation or chemotherapy—once we know exactly what kind of tumor we're dealing with."

He turns to Mason. "Okay, buddy. Let's see how you're doing. Can you close your eyes and touch your finger to your nose?"

This time Mason touches his nose without joking.

"Now close your eyes and hold your hands out in front of you."

Mason's hands shake, the right more than the left. It's the usual neurological test, with the usual results.

"That's good, Mason, thank you. I bet you're wondering what's going to happen with this tumor in your head."

"Yeah," Mason says quietly.

The doctor smiles and runs his fingers through Mason's long brown hair. "The surgeon is going to cut a window in your skull and take the tumor out," he says, his voice registering oddly cheerful.

Mason begins to sob. Alan and I huddle around him, holding him, while the oncologist mouths, "You need to prepare yourselves."

He means we could lose Mason. I can tell by the way he pulls his brow into what he estimates is an appropriate expression of sympathy. I suspect that Dr. Alba has saved his share of the children whose smiling faces adorn the bulletin board in the reception area. He has an impossible job, no doubt. But despite his qualifications and possible "good" intention to protect his colleague by convincing us to stop second-guessing Mason's missed diagnosis, he's not the doctor for us.

Alan excuses himself. I know where he's going: to start calling pediatric neurosurgeons and find the one who is.

Less than an hour later, we're driving across the Bay Bridge toward Oakland. The sky above us is sweatshirt gray, the water below the same cold, sad shade. Dr. Peter Sun, a pediatric neurosurgeon, is waiting for us at his office. When Alan reached him, Dr. Sun said he'd meet us at noon, even though his office is closed for the day. A red-haired woman about my age meets us at the door.

"I'm Beverly, the office manager," she says, motioning for us to come in.

The overhead lights are off, but sunlight filters through the windows. The walls are covered with thank-you notes, drawings, and photographs of smiling children. Beverly offers Mason a handful of mini Hershey bars and suggests they play name-that-tune on her iPod while Alan and I talk to the doctor.

Dr. Sun is in his forties, Asian, with long hair, kind eyes, and slim fingers. He looks like he might run marathons when he isn't saving children's lives. Silently, he loads Mason's MRI into his computer. He clicks through the images one by one.

"This is the internal capsule." Dr. Sun points to a structure that runs through Mason's brain. "This is where a number of critical motor and sensory fibers travel through the cortex, controlling vision, movement, walking, talking, swallowing. You can see how Mason's tumor has wrapped itself around it."

I want to put my head between my knees. Alan looks ashen.

"This tumor isn't something that I'd want to try to remove. The potential for damage is too great."

My mind skids. I don't like the idea of leaving something in Mason's brain that isn't supposed to be there. Then again, not having a big brain surgery is good news. Maybe. Dr. Sun agrees that the tumor has probably been there Mason's entire life. He speculates that it's a slow-growing variety.

"A biopsy will tell us what kind of tumor this is, so we can treat it." His voice is calm and sure. "The surgery requires making a couple of small holes in Mason's skull and a few days in the hospital."

Mason, already cheered by the Hershey bars (obviously chocolate wasn't his real problem), looks even happier now as Beverly leads him into the office where Dr. Sun assures him that there will be no windows in his skull, just two or three tiny holes.

# seven

# When the Walls Come Down

By the time Mason got his diagnosis, we'd started fixing up our old house and had moved into a rental three miles from home—a boxy, three-bedroom built in the 1960s that reminds me, in a good way, of the houses I grew up in.

The renovation wasn't elective. Our house had charm, history, and fifteen years of deferred maintenance. The plywood patch in the kitchen floor will finally be repaired with real wood, and we'll get rid of the 1980s skylights that leak pine needles onto the kitchen counters whenever the wind blows. Two weeks ago, that was my biggest worry. Now I don't care if paint is peeling off of my windowsills. (I've already lead-tested it.)

My first days of being the mother of a child with a brain tumor have passed. I'm four pounds lighter, and I have swollen eyes over gaunt cheekbones. I look like an older, heavy-drinking version of myself, even though the strongest sedative I allow myself is Yogi Bedtime tea.

Five days before Mason's biopsy, my mother arrives with a meaty casserole. (After our short stint as vegetarians ten years ago, she still feels it's her duty to make sure my kids get their fill of iron and pro-tein.) I asked her to come. I want to have her here for my kids, as I'm too much of a jumbled mess, and I worry that they need more than I can give.

"Hi, Grandma." Austin hugs my mom and hangs on for a moment or two, even though he's thirteen. His blond bangs are long, so I can't read his expression. I wipe my eyes with the heel of my hand. Growing up I'd learned to stomp out inconvenient and scary feelings that threatened my ability to maintain control (i.e., survive) amid the chaos. This is a skill I've honed as an adult, a superpower I use to run the business of our family with a mostly affectionate efficiency. The problem is I now find myself leaking—all the time.

Mom hands me a tissue. She's known to carry them in her pockets and rolled into her sleeves. I'm reassured by her presence, the arch of her eyebrow, and the shopping bag filled with Ziploc containers.

"Stop crying," eight-year-old Sarah tells me in a tone mothers use with their whining children. Ordinarily, that would make me laugh, but I'm afraid that I'm losing my ability to cope: laughter, tears, whatever, whenever. I reach down and pick up Sarah. Her feet dangle around my knees.

"I'm okay," I tell her. "Sometimes things that happen make me sad. But the only thing we know for sure is that everything changes. Even the scary things won't stay that way forever." I remember how my mom's tears scared me. I'd already started to buoy myself when I was Sarah's age. I hope my tears show my daughter that she can survive big feelings, that they won't consume her. I pray it's true.

"Sarah, look what I've brought you." Mom pulls the lid off a container of chocolate chip cookies. I appreciate that her husband, Art, was also willing to come. His big personality will be a gift to Mason, who has already set up his Dog-Opoly version of Monopoly in anticipation of the visit. Art drapes a loose arm around me in a quick hug.

I knew my mom would come when I needed her, and that every other annoyance would fall away. "Take some time for yourself," she says as the kids help her unload.

Mom was almost twenty-one when I was born. We've grown up side by side, devoted, loving and irritating each other in a mostly positive ratio. Healing in our family began when we started telling the truth. I would've preferred to hopscotch over this part, the grief and anger, the risky, uncomfortable words that had to be spoken. But we didn't give up. Each of us had work to do, but we'd get through.

I tell Alan I'm going to drive over to the house and see what's up. He's in the bedroom working on a spreadsheet, getting his job done when he can these days. He's already missed a lot of work.

"Do you want me to come with you?" he asks. His eyes are flat, as if the vital part of him has retreated while he focused on his screen.

"It's okay," I say. "I can use some time to myself." Alan pushes his chair away from the table and pulls me onto his lap.

"I hate this," I say.

"I know," he answers. He does know—he's the only one who knows.

We just celebrated our fifteenth wedding anniversary with a weekend at San Francisco's Plaza Hotel. We wandered through our favorite neighborhoods like in our early days, when all we had was time, and we couldn't seem to get enough of it together. That Saturday morning we walked down Fillmore Street, warming our hands on coffee cups, the way we used to. This might have sustained us until Thanksgiving, if only our children's biggest health problem was still an occasional case of strep throat.

Alan tears up. I turn away because it reminds me of my own terror and sadness, which threaten to topple me. I want to be close to my husband, but any extra energy I have goes to the kids, especially now. It feels necessary and wrong at the same time.

"I'd better get going before the sun sets," I say as I kiss him goodbye, an efficient, quick peck.

"See you soon," he says, and returns his determined focus to the computer screen.

From the front, our house looks the same. The peaked roof with the brown Tudor trim, blooming pink camellias lining the stone path to the door. It occurs to me that I could drive back to our temporary house, load the cat, the two dogs, and laundry baskets filled with dishes into the minivan, move us back into our real house, and pretend that nothing bad had happened. I could hit rewind on the series of doctors' appointments, the MRI, and the scheduled biopsy, the way Wonder Woman spun the Earth in reverse when she'd missed the opportunity to prevent the actual tragedy. All we need to do is return to how it was two weeks ago.

I walk around to the back of the house. It is gone. No walls. Half a roof. No kitchen. All that's left of our old life is the facade, the bare floors, some metal beams, wooden posts, and scaffolding. It's like a dollhouse I had when I was young, the back removed so I could move the mother, father, brother, and sister figures from room to room, where they would sit stiffly on plastic chairs, each of them with satisfied painted-on smiles.

I love our house, the trees. Alan and I have come a long way. And we still fall short regularly even on the days we look our shiniest on Facebook. It might help that we keep praying together, asking for strength that isn't limited by our exhaustion and pettiness. We share a life full of things and people to disagree about. We blame each other for how hard things get, how tired we are. We argue, we stew, and we come back together. It hasn't been easy but, so far, underneath any hurt feelings, we've unearthed the bond that brought us together, that keeps us together. We choose each other one more time, every time. I hope it's enough.

The sun recedes behind the tree-lined ridge, casting long shadows. I cross my arms against the chill, and the contractor's phrase comes to mind.

"We're in the demolition stage," he said, and he was right.

*eight*

# As the Reflex Takes Over

It's been nine days since Dr. Sun extracted cells from the tumor through two small burr holes in Mason's skull. When he woke up, Mason was joking with the nurse, his voice hoarse from the anesthesia. "I'm loopy." He laughed, his mood defiant and cheerful. I laughed, too, and then I cried alone in the hospital bathroom. The tumor cells were sent to a lab in Los Angeles. It was supposed to take five to seven days for the pathologist to come up with a diagnosis, but every afternoon I'm told "maybe tomorrow."

Mason is back at school along with his brother and sister; Alan is in his office. And I'm home alone with my awful thoughts. Trying not to jump to horrible conclusions is like trying not to throw up when the reflex takes over. A Buddhist friend tells me I have a two-headed dog, and it is my choice which head to feed. I know it's smarter to feed the happy, positive dog, the one without the mange of disaster and doom. But I don't always have the willpower to resist giving the bad dog a rub. (At least with him I won't be caught unaware and unprepared.)

My friend Annie offered to pray with me every day. She also lent me her porcelain Magnificent Mary medal, which I wear on a gold chain around my neck. I'm supposed to return it to her when the crisis passes. A not-desperately-needy friend would have returned the necklace already. But these weeks are stretching long, and being my prayer buddy takes on the quality of an endurance sport.

"It's me," I say when she answers the phone.

"How did the night go?" she asks.

"The usual. I was up from two to five. I haven't felt so tired since I had babies."

"Intensive self-care," she reminds me. "Eat a good breakfast. Go for a walk."

Then we pray. Or rather, Annie prays and I uh-huh, sniffle, and rub the Mary charm.

"God, we pray for Mason's healing. We know You've got this; that the solution is already in process. But it's a scary time for mothers. Please help Janine through the day, give her the strength she needs, and the grace."

My neediness is embarrassing. As a person who devoted her life to being super capable, it's particularly unsettling. I feel relief when Annie is on the other end of the phone. Eventually, though, we have to hang up, and I'm left with me. But this morning, instead of trying not to think about what might be going wrong in Mason's brain, I shift my focus to the neurologist who "forgot" to order an MRI during Mason's era of "migraines" and "normal" tremors. I also think of Dr. Window-In-The-Head scouring Mason's chart for what I'd done wrong, anything that could absolve the hospital and his colleague of liability. Had I breastfed him long enough? Vacationed near Chernobyl?

I hold Dr. B.'s business card in one hand, the phone in the other. I dial Mom instead.

"What do you want to get out of this?" she asks.

"I want her to feel bad," I answer. My mood lifts at the thought of someone else shouldering this heaviness, the blame.

"Sure you do, but where do you want to put your energy right now?"

This seems like a better place to focus my energy than imagining Mason's empty bedroom. But I concede Mom might have a point. I don't call Dr. B. after we hang up. I put it off like sober friends do a drink . . . *maybe tomorrow.*

I move a pile of folded clothes so I can sit on the couch. There's a certain cruelty to the brightness outside the window, the view of the yellowed grass on the hillside and the black road below, as if Mother Earth doesn't notice that the flashy blue sky burns my tired eyes. I curl into a ball on the clean laundry. The marrow-sucking worry and the lack of sleep leave me completely empty.

Alan and I are in Dr. Sharp's office, waiting for the results of Mason's biopsy. Dr. Sharp (not his actual name) is a pediatric neuro-oncologist who specializes in treating children's brain tumors. A tall, bald man, Dr. Sharp shakes our hands, then leads us into a small exam room in the back of the oncology clinic. He offers us each a chair, then hoists himself onto the examination table, his navy slacks creasing the sanitary paper.

"Do you want to meet Mason?" I ask. Mason is waiting in the reception area with my friend Joan.

"Not necessary," Dr. Sharp says. "I've looked at his MRI."

It was a mistake to pull Mason out of school for this appointment. Missing class is never good, especially when I've convinced myself that this brain tumor thing is a detour, a pit-stop. We need to keep normal close by so we can merge back in when the time comes.

"We don't have the pathology results yet," Dr. Sharp says.

I want to scream. The biopsy results are four days late, days that stretch like dog years, one impossible moment of not knowing after another. My hands ball into fists in my lap.

"I have a call in to the pathologist," he continues. "It's a large mass. I'm quite sure about the course of treatment. Your son will need fifty-eight weeks of chemotherapy. It won't make the tumor go away, but it has a 70 percent chance of stopping its growth."

I can't break down, and I can't wrap my mind around this information. I form the shapes of letters with my pen, recording the names of the drugs in a black-and-white composition book I bought just for these notes. I put a pink heart sticker on the front cover that says "You are loved" so I can remember that there's a God who loves me, though I'm not feeling it right now.

"How will chemotherapy affect his fertility?" I'm in reporter mode, impressive in my calm. No fainting, hysterical mother here. I see Mason's handsome face, the thick brown hair, the skin, like mine, a sallow shade easily browned. I imagine the girl who will love him one day. Dr. Sharp doesn't appear to hear me.

"We've been using this combination of drugs on children for thirty years with good results, good survival rates."

"Couldn't the tumor be benign?" I choke out.

"We don't consider anything growing in a child's brain benign," Dr. Sharp says. "It's cancer."

"What about immunotherapy?" Alan asks. He has researched this cutting-edge treatment, which uses a patient's cancer cells to create a vaccine that fights the tumor.

"Still in the experimental stage," Dr. Sharp answers. "Mason's tumor is too large for the gamma knife. Conventional radiation would render him a vegetable."

*Mason? Bright, funny Mason—a vegetable?*

"If you don't act now, your son will be dead in two years." His words hang in the air.

There seems to be a wall in my mind that won't let the words through; instead they tumble to the ground, like alphabet blocks. I will pick them up later. I will understand when I'm able.

His phone rings, and he excuses himself and walks out of the room. When the door closes behind him, I force an awkward inhale. "Please, God, make it all a big mistake," I pray.

Dr. Sharp returns and reclaims his seat on the exam table. The fingers that grip my poised pen feel like they're attached to someone else's hand.

"Good news," Dr. Sharp says. "The pathologist said it's a neuroglioma, grade II, much better than it looked from the scans."

Two pieces of information fight it out in my head. My son has brain cancer. And yet somehow this is good news.

"This is a slow-growing tumor," he confirms. "But it's already so large, there's no room for it to grow without putting excessive pressure on critical brain structures. My recommendation stands—fifty-eight weeks of chemotherapy over the next three years, starting immediately."

Alan puts his hand over mine. My hand is numb, like the rest of me.

"Is it possible the tumor has already stopped growing?" Alan asks in a respectful, good-student voice.

Dr. Sharp stops tapping his Bally loafers against the side of the exam table and looks Alan in the eye. "That kind of thinking will kill your child."

Alan's hand goes icy in mine. "Okay," he says grimly. "Let's schedule the next appointment."

We all stand up. Dr. Sharp puts one hand on Alan's shoulder, the other hand on mine. "Don't forget to take care of your relationship," he says cheerfully. "Get some time for yourselves. Plan a weekly date."

"Thank you," we say in unison. We don't let ourselves register any condescension. We can't. Our dominant emotion is terror, registered through layers of held-breath numbness. We are good parents. We will do whatever it takes to save Mason.

# nine

# Quiet, Clear Yes

I don't like it, but I resign myself to Dr. Sharp's brand of chemotherapy. We're doing the right thing—or something, anyway. I convince myself that Dr. Sharp's protocol will save Mason's life, that there's no other choice. Then the phone rings.

"This is Paul Fisher from Stanford returning your call."

It might as well be Mick Jagger. Dr. Fisher is Stanford Children's Hospital's neuro-oncologist—not a scheduler, an intern, or a nurse. I called him because I'm doing my due diligence, getting a second opinion, even though I don't expect it to change anything, because if you don't get a second opinion for this, what would you get one for?

"Dr. Sharp recommends fifty-eight weeks of chemo to make sure the tumor stops growing," I explain.

"How do you know the tumor hasn't already stopped growing?" he asks. "Fifty percent of these tumors stop growing on their own."

Dr. Fisher's voice is unemotional but kind. This is apparently a statement of fact. It's also the question that keeps coming into Alan's mind every time he sits quietly or pauses in his day. He can't seem to make the question go away, even after Dr. Sharp warned that these subversive thoughts could kill Mason. I scribble "50% stop growing" on the back of an envelope.

"I can't make any recommendation without examining Mason," Dr. Fisher continues, "but I can tell you that a lot of families regret rushing into treatment. You might very well decide to do the chemo, but there's no rush with this pathology. This is a slow-growing tumor."

"We'll bring Mason to see you," I say. "Thank you."

I call Alan, happier than I can remember ever being.

The initial appointment with Dr. Fisher goes well, at least that's how I see it. He recommends we monitor the tumor and delay any treatment until (or if) the tumor grows or changes. It's good news. Alan and I tag teamed brilliantly through the day, converging from different freeways to arrive at the children's hospital, then diverging again, his work, and my pick-ups, drop-offs, and finally dinner together. We haven't had a real conversation about this course change, but it's obviously the right move, a miracle even.

"Do you want to call Dr. Sharp's office and tell them Mason's not going to do the chemo? Or should I?" I ask once the kids are in bed.

"Whoa! I never said I wanted to cancel the chemo," Alan says. "What if Mason's tumor *is* growing?"

It hadn't occurred to me that Alan could be so wrong at such a critical time. "You've been asking the same question Dr. Fisher asked, 'What if the tumor has stopped growing?' We've been praying for a miracle. And here's a coincidence: one of the top neuro-oncologists asking the same thing, using the same exact words. It's got to be a God Thing." My voice sounds shrill, even to my own ears.

"I'm not comfortable with that decision." Alan chops his words into cold, cutting bites. "I don't even know if I trust this guy." Alan's rational tone sounds like a deliberate attack, a strategy to win. Plus, he's wrong and possibly out of his mind.

"You didn't like Sharp either," I snap back. "And he based his entire diagnosis on the scans even before we had pathology reports. He didn't bother to examine Mason."

"I'm not ready to make a decision." Alan slams his laptop closed and walks out of the room.

I'm sure that I'm right and he's wrong. How could Alan not see this was a great day? The way Dr. Fisher extended his hand to Mason first. How he took in Mason's standard uniform, a Giants T-shirt and a matching SF hat. "The Giants?" said the smiling doctor with salt-and-pepper hair and sweater vest. "Really?"

Who knew this revered pediatric neuro-oncologist was an A's fan? We all laughed too loudly and too long as I vowed that we would be the most agreeable, fun-loving family Dr. Fisher ever saved.

"What sports do you like to play?" Dr. Fisher asked in a string of questions that I quickly realized were part of the exam.

"I like basketball. I used to play baseball, but it got too hard with my tremor." Mason held out his hands that shook predictably.

"So now you mostly watch baseball on TV?" the doctor asked as he shone a pen light in each of Mason's eyes.

"Yeah. Go, Giants!"

"Have you seen the pathology report?" Alan asked him.

"Yes, and we talked about Mason in Tumor Board this morning," Dr. Fisher answered. The Tumor Board meets once a week and includes the radiologists (who read the scans), pathologists (who examine tissue samples), neurosurgeons, radiation oncologists, and neuro-oncologists like Dr. Fisher who manage the overall treatment plan.

"Today's exam shows how well Mason's brain has adapted to the mass, and how astonishingly well he functions. If you just looked at the size of the mass, you might think this boy is completely debilitated."

I wanted to throw myself into Dr. Fisher's arms. This has been my point all along: Mason is amazingly healthy, smart, articulate, zany, and strong—except for the tumor.

"So what do you recommend we do?" Alan asked.

"To start with, let's remember that this is a low-grade lesion, and half of them won't change over the years. Half do. At this point in time we don't know if it's growing," Dr. Fisher said. "We typically scan every three months."

"What about chemo?" Alan asked in his work voice, the one that formulates plans and calculates risk.

"Right now I would recommend against it. It's likely that in Mason's lifetime, this tumor will need to be treated. But I'd like to give his body and his brain a chance to mature as much as possible before we intervene."

It's the best news we've had in weeks, and now my husband refuses to let it in the door. I call Joan.

"I hate this," I cry. "We had a great appointment. It was a total God Thing. And Alan still won't call off the chemo plan with Dr. Doom."

To be clear, a "God Thing" is something that moves us in the direction of my acceptable storyline, meaning that Mason will live the long, happy life I've planned for him, and not undergo any treatment that causes pain or makes him sick.

"Alan's terrified," Joan explains. "You're desperate for a savior, and right now his name is Dr. Fisher. Alan's too scared to believe there is one, lest he let his guard down and something really awful happens."

"Yeah, well, he needs to get over it," I say.

Joan sighs. "You're in an impossible situation—both of you. You'll find your way. You always have."

I'm not so sure. Alan and I fall asleep angry. And when I hear his footsteps as he leaves at five a.m., I roll over and sleep for two more hours. We don't talk during the day. I am chopping up vegetables for a stir-fry when he gets home from work. We forgo our usual kiss hello, both of us still achy and misunderstood.

"How was your day?" I ask by rote.

"Busy," he says. "I talked to Dr. Fisher."

"What? Why did you call him?"

"He said to call with any questions, and I had some. I asked him about the MRI plan. He said it would be fine to scan Mason in eight weeks to start out with instead of twelve, and I have his direct number in case we have any problems before then."

"Wow, that's great," I say. "So you're ready to call off the chemo for now?"

"Yeah. But do you mind calling Dr. Sharp's office and letting them know? I have a board meeting tomorrow."

After dinner, I'm catching up on e-mail when Alan comes into the kitchen and kisses the top of my head. "Do you want to go for a walk?" he asks.

We cross the street onto the trail that starts at the end of the block. To our right we look down on Highway 101; to our left is open space, a brown hillside wrapped in tall yellow grasses, dotted with coastal live oaks. Some of the oaks are green and sturdy, but others are shorn into pieces, limbs collapsed, eaten from the inside out by Sudden Oak Death, a scourge that has been clearing hillsides and backyards for the past five years. Alan reaches for my hand.

"I'm not trying to make this harder on you than it already is. I just need to get to know the Stanford people before I'm all in. What if they got the pathology wrong and the tumor keeps growing? What if we miss a chance to stop it? What if we make the wrong decision and Mason pays for it?"

"I get it," I say. "But it's working out. I think it's all a sign, doors opening and all."

I'm not disagreeing with Alan, and I hope this reassures him. I've heard enough to support the knowing that comes from the center of myself; the quiet, clear "yes."

*ten*

# The Unseen Reptile

Under the watchful eye of Dr. Fisher and the Stanford Pediatric Tumor Board, we seize our fragile reprieve: Mason is to have no chemo and no surgeries right now, unless he comes down with a blinding headache and stiff neck (hydrocephalus), or if he begins to tremor more, or worst case, if something unseen reveals itself. We will attempt to live life on these strange new terms like we know what we're doing, as if we haven't been catapulted out of the comfortable, safe place we thought was our habitat.

Having survived up until now by my personal creed of anticipating trouble and girding against it (i.e., trying to control everything), living with this uncertainty is like asking me to cohabitate with an unseen reptile. The lurking feeling that I had as a child is back. Danger is under the couch, in the dark corners of the closet, or in that boot I haven't worn since last February. A feeling of never being safe has replaced the illusion of safety that came from what was apparently a one-sided agreement with God: that I would be the very best mom, daughter, citizen, churchgoer, driver, and sober woman, and my kids might not get eaten alive.

Friends remind me that I have just this one day to live. *Cute.* When I first heard about this approach, as a newly sober person, I conceded it was the best strategy for those poor alcoholics who had trouble planning ahead. I was different. I'd admit that on a bad day I just had to root for bedtime, but mostly I worked hard to get ahead, exercised when I didn't feel like it, contributed to my IRA, and bought the appropriate insurance. Right now, I'm forced into this "just for today" attitude, but I put my own spin on it . . . *Just for today, I will figure out how to cure Mason's tumor.*

Time is a blessing, a chance to attack the tumor on other fronts. Although my mind is open to conventional treatments, my not-so-secret hope is to unearth a miracle cure. It seems reasonable that if we can boost Mason's immune system, maybe it can knock out the tumor on its own. Of course it hasn't done so yet, but that might be because we haven't found the right fortifications.

This opens the fun house door because if beating Mason's brain tumor is as simple as cutting out sugar, nitrates, and food additives, does it follow that jelly beans and pepperoni caused it in the first place? Doubtful, but there's the seesaw of blame, cause, and cure. Everything is suspect, and I'm responsible for most of it.

One of Mason's oncologists told me, "This isn't about the glass of wine you had when you were pregnant." But I didn't have a glass of wine when I was pregnant. No whiskey. No raw fish, aspartame, dental X-rays, or secondhand smoke. I ate my vegetables, and when Mason was old enough, he did too. If this could happen to us, well, it could happen to anyone. Except maybe the strict vegans. We didn't try that. And the six months we spent as ice cream–swilling vegetarians apparently doesn't count.

I think about the summer when I was seventeen, when my friends and I raced between one another's houses at dusk to avoid the approaching helicopters spraying our backyards to prevent a medfly invasion that would've been catastrophic to California agriculture. The next morning I'd swim laps in the pool. The cat would roll in the grass, then fall asleep on my bed. We might as well have slathered ourselves in chemicals, which, in fact, we did during those childhood Chicago summers, hoping to keep the mosquitos away. What if I hadn't weaned Mason when I did? The hamster wheel whirls; one incriminating thought leads to the next. If I could only understand why and how, I'm convinced I'll gain advantage over the tumor. The only relief is to outrun it.

I make appointments, and I drive Mason to all of them with plenty of water and blood sugar–stabilizing organic almonds in the car. We see Dr. Azzolino twice a week. His chiropractic adjustments and exercises calm Mason's tremor, and Mason gets fewer headaches. His writing and drawing improve. He knits Alan a scarf. He hides any fear behind the shock value he's found in the words "I have brain cancer."

"How are you feeling?" I ask him.

"There's not really a word for it," he says. "But it's a pretty good way to get attention."

There's a vein of sadness underneath Mason's jokes. A distance is emerging between him and his formerly close friends as he spends more time away from school. He's tired a lot. He misses a birthday party when he has one of his headaches. His new companions are adults—therapists, doctors, nurses, and, of course, me, his mom.

For years I've walked past a nearby alternative medicine clinic, vaguely aware that they help people with cancer. Now my son is one of those people.

"This will be really great," I tell Mason as we sit in the waiting room. "They're experts on making people's bodies strong to fight tumors."

"Cool," Mason replies. "But can we please get some gluten-free cookies at the bakery?" This is what you'd expect from a ten-year-old boy, but things, of course, aren't usual for us anymore.

"I thought you liked almonds," I remind him, pulling the baggie from my purse. Alan takes the plastic bag from me. *He* likes almonds.

When my mother-in-law, Janice, explained how cancer cells go wild on PET scans when injected with radioactive sugar, I decided to cut sugar out of our diet. I baked a batch of gluten-free peanut butter cookies sweetened with the smallest amount of maple syrup. I thought they were delicious, but the kids were less than thrilled. Austin took one bite and asked, "Do we have any ice cream?"

"Mom, I have a brain tumor," Mason adds. "I should be able to eat whatever I want."

I roll my eyes. Alan shrugs.

The shelves that line the walls in the waiting room are jammed with jars of herbs, bright boxes of teas, and books on nutrition and cancer. Two standard poodles doze near the door. They're trained to sniff out melanoma, so I'm relieved when they take a polite but indifferent attitude toward us.

We're greeted by Michael, a Chinese medicine master who looks more like a Haight-Ashbury hippie with his shoulder-length hair, loose T-shirt, and faded jeans. He offers us each a cup of green tea, then ushers us into his office.

"They say he's probably had the tumor his entire life," I explain, and hand Michael a copy of the pathology report.

"We put off chemo for the time being," Alan adds.

"Our hope is that it's stopped growing," I say. "While we wait and see, we're treating it from an alternative perspective. But there's so much out there, it's hard to know where to start."

Michael nods, flipping through the report. "I'll put together a personalized plan based on Mason's diagnosis," he says. "I'll give you a list of different oncology options, along with practitioners who might be able to help. I'll also recommend supplements and therapies. After twenty-five years I know who and what you can trust."

Two weeks later we're back in Michael's office, sipping green tea while he reads to us from a ten-page plan: a Brazilian oncologist working on a Dendritic cell vaccine, a nutritionist in Utah who's done extensive research on brain tumors, researchers at Duke University, and a contact at the Neurosurgical Institute at Cedars-Sinai, for a second opinion about surgical resection. There's also a list of fruits, vegetables, and nuts that Mason should be eating, along with a regimen of supplements to strengthen his immune system.

I leave with a brown paper bag filled with stubby bottles of supplements. Now there's something I can do. Or rather, now there are some things I'll be forcing Mason to do. It's a huge relief.

Michael suggested that we call Dr. Mark Renneker, a physician and medical school professor who helps families navigate complex medical diagnoses. Dr. Renneker created a groundbreaking university course called the "Biology of Cancer," and wrote the textbook *Understanding Cancer*. In Mason's opinion, his most important qualification is that "Dr. Mark" is a well-known big-wave hunter, a world-class surfer who travels the globe in pursuit of huge waves. He's just back from surfing off glaciers somewhere when we speak for the first time.

"I'd say the first step is to get a second opinion on the pathology. All of your decisions stem from the type of tumor and its grade, so you want to be very sure about this," he says. "As for the supplements, you should check anything you give Mason to make sure it's copper-free. There's some research showing that brain tumors thrive on copper."

"Is there anything we're missing?" Alan asks.

"I've had a few patients work with a psychotherapist named Christopher. He gets amazing results using creative visualization. I have a fifty-year-old client with a brain tumor, and she calls him her secret weapon."

The following Tuesday morning, I pull Mason out of his weekly violin class to take him to Christopher's office. Christopher is young, in his late twenties maybe, with a monastic look: shaved head, gentle eyes, and an austere office. A tabletop fountain makes a bubbling noise that almost masks the voices within the adjacent therapy room.

"How are you doing, Mason?" Christopher asks.

"Well, I have brain cancer," Mason says cheerfully.

"It's a tumor," I interject. "Not a high-grade tumor that people normally associate with the word *cancer*. He's probably had it his entire life."

I can't stop Mason from using the *cancer* word, which scares me, as if by saying it, he's willing his tumor to become more virulent, and by not saying it, I'm in denial.

"I almost had to have chemo," Mason says. "So it's cancer."

"But it's not what people think of as cancer that spreads through your body," I say because I just can't let it go. Then I remember that we're talking to a psychotherapist and I smile, embarrassed.

"It sounds really challenging," Christopher says neutrally.

"It sucks," Mason says, squishing his face into a silly grin.

"I bet it does," Christopher says. "I've worked with lots of kids who are dealing with stuff just like you, Mason."

"Cancer?"

"Yes, cancer. And other things too—injuries, other diseases."

Christopher passes Mason's first test. Unlike me, he doesn't squirm, cry, or appear excessively worried when Mason uses the *C* word.

"I'll wait in the other room so you guys can talk," I say, demonstrating that I'm a mom who knows proper limits and boundaries.

I'm studying Michael's list of "foods to avoid" when Mason emerges from Christopher's office.

"How'd it go?"

"Great. I like this guy." Mason looks back over his shoulder at Christopher, who's standing behind him.

"I like this guy too," Christopher says with a broad smile. "I think we're going to do some good work together." The two of them exchange high fives. I hand Christopher a check.

"I'm learning to use lasers and light sabers on my tumor." Mason laughs as we climb into the car. And that's all he chooses to share. What happens in Christopher's office stays in Christopher's office.

We're given a pass at Mason's MRI appointment. "Boring," proclaims Dr. Fisher, "and in this clinic, that's a good thing."

Days add up to months, the tumor appears to hibernate while I build what blockades I can. I fill my grocery cart with apples, whose skins contain twelve anticancer elements. I pick out tomatoes rich in lycopene, a phytochemical with powerful antitumor effects. Maybe it's all working. Maybe.

Mason writes a report on brain tumors. He says, "Brain tumors are like snakes. Not all of them are deadly."

# eleven

# Awkward Prayer

All over the world people are praying for Mason, sanctuaries of every flavor in nearly every state and on several continents, including school children in Myanmar and a group in the state prison where our friend Jack volunteers. Annie has lit candles for Mason in churches in Egypt and Thailand. I'm sure it helps, every word, every loving intention.

People who claim enlightenment sometimes say, "God doesn't give you more than you can handle." But I can't handle this, at least not on my own.

We started attending Annie's church, St. Andrew Presbyterian in Marin City, a small congregation nestled against the hills on the north side of Golden Gate National Park. I had my reasons for the break up with the religion of my childhood, though I still cross myself with holy water whenever it's offered. I returned Annie's Miraculous Mary medal, but only after she gifted me one of my own, which I never take off. These days I'm layering it with a green felt Blessed Virgin scapular bought at the Mission gift shop where they sell cheap but grace-filled souvenirs.

I pray most mornings and meditate when I can tolerate sitting quietly with my thoughts. I've always believed in a Higher Power that makes the daffodils bloom every spring, that Bigger Resource I ask for sobriety, strength, and healthy children.

Therein lies the problem. A sick child seems to mean the system is flawed; that only certain mothers' prayers are answered. I need a bigger God, a place to pray, question, and sometimes cry. Annie's church fits. It's a "come as you are" kind of place. Like me, people struggle with life on life's terms and come to church speaking that simple prayer: "Help."

This particular Sunday, I'm sitting alone in the second row. It's a rare moment for me, a time when I can just *be*.

Pastor Veronica is an African American woman in a stylish skirt-suit, and looks nothing like the gowned male priests of my childhood. "I hear people say that they're 'doing well under the circumstances.' The point of prayer is to get above the circumstances. To tap into the joy that is always there, no matter what the circumstances." She pauses for a sip of water. "Is there anyone who needs a special prayer today?"

I shrug off my embarrassment at being seen in my needy unkempt state and walk to the altar. The exhaustion is getting to me. Three people stand with me: Luke, who drags a canister of oxygen behind him, the cannula under his nose sustaining him because his own lungs are failing. Patti, slim with a graying bob, who just lost her job. And Marrieta, with dark hair in a neat bun. She works at San Quentin, which must be difficult even on the best days.

Pastor Veronica approaches each of us in turn, pausing as Luke, then Patti, then Marrieta whisper into her ear. When she leans into me, I whisper, "Sustenance."

I worry that I'm becoming a prayer hog. I've put myself in this spot every Sunday for months now, starting with the first time Alan and I stood here crying while Veronica and the people of St. Andrew prayed for Mason's survival.

"We pray for Mason's continued healing and for his family's strength and peace of mind. We know God is able."

After we've returned to our seats, Pastor Veronica closes the service. "I want you to stand up," she tells the congregation. "Look at your hands."

I hold my hands out in front of me. My nails are clipped short, my cuticles ragged.

"Now look at your arms," she says, "and your feet."

I inspect the sleeves of my sweater and my dusty Converse.

"Jesus has no other hands, no other feet, no other arms. Go out and do what He would have you do. Love and serve the Lord."

This boost of acceptance and love feels like a thick sweatshirt on a foggy morning, something lent by a friend. There's that hopeful feeling of burrowing into the generosity, of warmth against skin chilled by the elements. I find it in this sanctuary and out in the world too, transmitted by people offering meals and carpool rides, the doctors who care deeply, the nurse with a steady hand on my shoulder, my mom, my dad. There is so much good, which we call God, here. I slide the hymnal back into its place underneath the pew, renewed for now anyway.

"Remember me?" a woman asks. Her halo of curls registers, but I can't place her. She isn't one of the regulars here.

"I'm Beth, Jessica's mom."

Austin and Jessica had been in a music class together ten years ago and became fast friends over tambourines and hand drums.

"Right." I smile. "How is she?"

"Good," she responds. Then she lowers her voice, "What's going on with Mason?"

Answering this question is always painful. But the sun is bright through the skylight above me; the coming cold rain will hold off for another day. I have just been blessed, and, in that moment, I feel openhearted.

"He has a brain tumor," I say.

Without a pause she blurts, "My college roommate Susan has one too. That's what brought me to church today and back to God. I haven't been here in years. Susan is going to have surgery next week. Her tumor is the size of a *quarter*."

I don't mention that we measure Mason's tumor in citrus fruit.

"I'm so sorry to hear that," I say. "Brain surgeons can do amazing things."

"How is Mason?" Beth asks, tears flowing down her cheeks.

"He's doing really well."

"I feel like I need to pray for him."

"That's wonderful. We love prayers." I hope my relaxed tone will calm her. Most of all, I hope it gets me away from her.

"It's just so tragic about Susan. She has terrible headaches. I haven't seen her for a long time, but I just can't stop thinking about her."

I don't notice Mason and Sarah entering the church with the Sunday school kids until they're right next to me, but Beth does.

"You probably don't remember me," Beth says to Mason. "Your brother and my daughter Jessica were friends back when you were a little guy."

Mason smiles and nods, with the distracted look that tells me he's ready for lunch. Sarah shoots me a matching look.

Beth's voice takes on the high squeak of a puppet on an early morning PBS show. "I want to pray for you. Is that okay?" She looks at me entreatingly.

I nod, hoping to get this over with so we can go home and eat leftover chili. I expect her to close her eyes and whisper a quick Presbyterian plea to the powers that be.

"What side is the tumor on?" she asks.

*Wait a minute*, I think. *Polite Presbyterian prayers do not require MRI mapping.* But I answer automatically. "It's on the left."

She positions her hands in Mason's hair. I freeze, my mouth gaping.

Her voice shifts from cloying to commanding, "Lord, I ask that You be with Mason. Heal him, Lord. I beg You to rid this boy of this invader. Cast out the sickness. We know this is not Your will, dear Lord. Heal this boy; relieve him."

Tears flow from Beth's eyes, and as she reaches up to dab them, Mason wriggles out from under her grasp. Sarah locks eyes with me, her expression inquiring whether we had all lost our minds while she was making clay crosses in the other room. This breaks the trance.

"Good to see you, Beth." I usher Mason and Sarah out the door.

When we're all seat-belted in the minivan with the doors locked, I turn to Mason.

"I'm so sorry. I didn't expect her to do that." I hate that I froze. That I didn't scream, "Hands off!" like a museum guard.

"That was weird." Mason laughs, thank God.

I believe in the power of what I can't see or understand. Something got me through when I was so empty, my human resources exhausted. A few thousand prayers sent our way during the most difficult moments cushioned and sustained us with a grace knit by the open-hearted goodness of others. We made it through one impossible day, then the next. But this was different. Beth was another mother, like me, who wished she could control more than is actually possible. She coughed her terror on us that Sunday morning, like someone who shouldn't be allowed to board the airplane. I wasn't feeling my own terror, not right then, not until she exhaled a fresh dose into Mason's messy hair.

Just the sight of me seems to remind people that their children are mortal, and this tends to freak them out. It freaks me out too. Beth isn't the only person to expose me to her viral load. Attempting to be a supportive wife, I attended one of Alan's business cocktail parties. I put on uncomfortable shoes and even applied eye shadow.

I was maneuvering a cube of chicken off a skewer when Henry approached. He'd worked with Alan for a year or so.

"I am so sorry about Mason," he said, breathing into my face.

"Thanks," I said, taking a big step backward.

"I think about him all the time. It's just so sad." He began to sob, then pulled me toward him in a one-sided embrace, dribbling his tears and the remnants of his vodka all over my silk blouse.

Everyone means well. But an interaction shifts into weird when the person providing the "comfort" needs more reassurance than I do, and their panic eclipses whatever I'm feeling in that moment. Right now, I feel a familiar urge to burrow behind the dresses in my closet, wrap my arms around my legs, and hide my head in the duck-and-cover posture. I'd been doing well, considering. Life had become almost predictable again, driving the kids to practice, making them do their homework. Of course, there are always Mason's appointments. I look at my calendar and get through each day one appointment at a time. Reactions like these momentarily make me forget where I am and what comes next. It reminds me that, no matter how many bottles of vitamins we empty, we live in a scary place still.

I drop off the kids at school on Monday morning and head into the grocery store. I run into an old friend, Marie, in the produce section. Her teenage son died in an accident two years ago. I push my cart over to where she's choosing apples.

"How are you? How's Mason?" she asks as we hug. I haven't seen Marie in a few months, but we share the same circle of friends so she knows what's been going on.

"I'm okay. We're not having to do anything about the tumor at this point. We're hoping it's something he'll just live with."

"I'm so glad to hear that," she says.

"I've been thinking about calling you," I speak slowly. "People are saying all kinds of strange things to me." I feel awkward, unsure of what I'm asking, hoping I hadn't been one of the many who, in unintentional ignorance, had said something off-key to Marie when Andrew died. "It throws me, having to deal with their stuff. I feel like I'm being pushed off balance. I remember you went through this kind of thing too."

"Yes," she says. I notice she looks better than she did the last time I saw her. She's gained back five pounds she couldn't spare to lose. She's calm.

"How did you deal with it?"

"I realized that there is no right thing to say."

We might be the hands and feet of God here on earth, but our human minds seem to go into overdrive trying to make sense of what doesn't make sense. I've gotten three e-mails from an acquaintance who insists that if I get the right kind of faith, Mason will be healed.

"There is no sickness in Jesus' perfect world!!!" she informs me with several enthusiastic exclamation points.

But it's like saying, if I grew another ear, Mason would be fine. I try. I really do, but I can't seem to make it happen. My faith feels fragile, flimsy, even prickly sometimes. I don't want to worry about whether Mason's next headache is ER worthy, whether the next scan will show something sinister. But the fear never really goes away.

Another friend offers, "You can't have fear and faith," as if I might just snap out of it. When I call my dad to share my annoyance, he says, "If you can't have fear and faith, what's courage?" We laugh, and I feel better.

I can't think my way out of the fear. I study spiritual books when I can't sleep, which is often. I listen to wise teachers. But it's like learning to dance. I can read all about it and watch helpful videos, but eventually I'll have to move my feet and try to catch the rhythm. Right now it seems the best I can hope for are short reprieves, moments when I don't feel so alone. It turns out that's enough to get me from one breath to the next.

*twelve*

# A New Solar System

I check off an endless to-do list that keeps me moving too fast to slip into the underground stream of anxiety that I can ignore except at night. Then the white noise is made audible in the silence, like the hum of a nearby freeway. When the sun rises, I say a prayer, then launch out of bed, letting the momentum of my needy family propel me through the day.

This morning I take a ride to meet Dries, the foreman at our real house, and make another list. I park next to the dumpster in the driveway, which gives me a full view of the house. I miss these redwoods that surround us—tall, still sentries. Dries is screwing a brass handle onto the pocket door he excavated from the living room wall.

"I took the hardware off and oiled and polished it at home last night. You can't replace this stuff," he says.

"Thank you." I appreciate that Dries understands this old house the way I do, like he's befriended the craftsman who hewed the original beams and spread thick plaster on the walls. It reassures me that our home has survived so much history, wars, earthquakes, and countless private tragedies. Like the tall trees overhead that shaded the Miwoks who gathered along the stream that once ran down the hill. There's shelter here; there always has been.

"We need you to decide on the tile, the bathroom fixtures, and the hardware this week," Dries says.

"No problem." *I'm back*, I think. Efficient, decisive, in charge.

⎯⎯⎯⎯

An hour later I hand the tile store salesman my list.

"Remodel?" he asks. "Boy, I feel for you. You know how high this ranks on the scale of stress? How hard it is on the relationship? I see it all the time. It's just brutal."

I nod. I do not say, "My son has a tumor the size of a lemon in his head. *That's* brutal." Instead I say, "I'd like to start with white subway tile."

The woman standing next to me looks a few years older than I am, and much better dressed, wearing a jacket that isn't waterproof. She holds a paint swatch up to the terra-cotta tile board mounted on the wall, then turns to her friend.

"I just can't decide," she says mournfully. "What am I going to do?"

I feel a pleasant glow of moral superiority to my well-dressed counterpart. I will not be losing sleep about whether my faucets are polished nickel or chrome. If Mason refuses to feel sorry for himself, I sure won't either. But I rethink the white tile. The terra-cotta the fancy lady found is pretty. I come home with a box of samples and catalogs.

I share my choices with Alan, and like the skilled mother I am, I narrow it down to two that I can live with.

"I like this bronze faucet," Alan says, flipping past my helpful pink Post-it notes marking acceptable choices.

"What? No!" I screech, hopeless at the thought of brass faucets clashing with the chrome tub filler. So much for perspective.

After dinner, Mason and Sarah chase our dog Moseley around the living room. The dog grabs a fruit leather out of Sarah's hand. He dodges Mason and runs through the open sliding-glass door onto the redwood deck. Eight-year-old Sarah runs after him, grabbing for his collar. She misses and trips. She holds up her hand to show us a toothpick-sized splinter in her palm. That's when the wailing begins. I pull Sarah onto my lap.

"It hurrrts," she cries.

"At least you don't have brain cancer," Mason says.

"Mason, that's *mean*." Sarah weeps.

"Well, it's not brain surgery," Mason says in his matter-of-fact way, as if Sarah might realize that she doesn't hurt that bad, wipe away the tears, and go back to chasing the dog.

"Stop it, Mason," she cries. "You're not the only one who gets hurt." She glares at her brother, then rolls her eyes at him like a much older girl.

These days if I want Mason to take out the garbage, he might answer, "Mom, I have brain cancer," while tightening his grip on the TV remote.

"Yes, you do. And you're going to take out the trash. What kind of mom would I be if I let you get away with that excuse?"

I'm making it up as I go, but it seems like "normal" is something we should aspire to, as in chores, bedtime, and equal attention to each child. But "normal" stays pinned to the horizon, always just a few miles down the road.

Even though I pretend it isn't true, our family orbits the tumor. It's a hostile and unpredictable solar system that's sucked us in. The minutia of the day anchors us in place, but it's impossible not to be affected. I'm in the school parking lot, waiting while Mason rehearses for the school play. But I see "it" the minute he walks out the doors. That faraway look, that heaviness. His step is slow, and he's slouched under the weight of his backpack. He opens the car door and slides his gear across the back seat.

"How are you, buddy?" I ask, though I already know.

"I have a headache."

"What number?" I ask, gauging whether I need to call Dr. Fisher.

"Seven," he says.

"When did it start?"

"After lunch."

I hand him my water bottle. He takes a sip and leans back against the headrest.

"I'll get you something as soon as we get home," I promise.

We keep the radio off and our voices down, bowing to Mason's headache. Silently, Austin stares outside. Sarah draws on an Etch A Sketch. Mason, eyes closed, rests his head against the window.

Today I give Mason his medicine and pull the shades in his room. I pour him a glass of cool water and urge him to drink. I call Trish, Dr. Fisher's nurse practitioner and watch for the tide to turn, one way or the other. And while I'm doing all of these things, I pray.

There are wars in Afghanistan and Iraq. Mothers are losing their children as "collateral damage." Soldiers, only five years older than Austin, come home without hands or feet, if they come home at all. Our family has no corner on suffering, but the tumor has exposed the unstable ground that's beneath us.

***

We move through the winter with fear suspended overhead like a Quentin-Tarantino-does-a-Road-Runner-cartoon. Mason goes to school and comes home with the usual headaches, the kind that go away with a dose of Tylenol and a good night's sleep.

And then, one rainy day in mid-March, the principal calls after lunch and asks me to pick him up.

"It's a bad one," Mason says while we drive to the hospital where our team is waiting for us in the ER. A CT scan confirms that the tumor has bled. CTs are better than MRIs at spotting blood. They also give off a troubling amount of radiation, but we do what we have to do. After Mason is settled with a dose of morphine and IV fluids, I call Alan, who's out of town, with the update.

"It's a bleed."

This messy tumor is sustained by a tangle of poorly laced blood vessels. The scan shows a small rupture in the tumor, but it looks like the bleeding has stopped. We'll spend the next two days in the hospital, making sure.

I tap into a channel of calm that enables me to form sentences, to recognize needs, to check things off. Alan secures a seat on an overnight flight from New York. He'll arrive in the morning. My dad picks up Sarah and Austin from school and makes them dinner. He will stay for as long as we need him. Mom spends the day with me at the hospital. She won't leave until she's sure I've eaten dinner.

Mason is moved into the PICU (Pediatric Intensive Care Unit) for the night. He sleeps, sedated and seemingly comfortable. I curl up on a sleeping recliner next to the bed. A baby shares this room with us. She's quiet, though her heartbeat is amplified through her monitor—a quick, constant mechanical beeping. I hear Mason's too, a cacophony of beats and buzzers, alarms that keep me from being able to sink down into myself, to doze off even though I'm exhausted.

Fear keeps me awake too. I'm afraid the tumor will blow. That we'll lose Mason. There's nothing I can do to get us out of the hospital and back to the "normal" I so carefully crafted out of our odd accumulation of circumstance. I pinch the Mary charm between my fingers, close my eyes, and pray "Hail Mary, full of grace," the prayer I learned in Sunday school all those years ago, before boys, before booze. When I come to the end of the prayer, I start again. I say the prayer fifty, a hundred times. My head aches from the tears welled up inside. Tears I stifle in front of Mason. Then when I can cry, like now, the tears are stuck, throbbing.

I'm tired of praying to a seemingly indifferent sky. I think Mary would understand. She agreed to the plan, a baby, a literal gift from God. This child grew into a man who challenged the way things always had been. He was loved and hated, anything but safe. She must've felt the terror of powerlessness, like other mothers—like me. But she held on another day. It wasn't passive acceptance reflected in her eyes; it was radical surrender and a willingness to keep an open heart. Hers was a no-matter-what faith big enough to hold it all.

"Holy Mary, mother of God, pray for us . . ."

The men who preached silent submission in my childhood churches might not have noticed the way the light played in her eyes through stained glass windows. The depth of the porcelain gaze that spoke of radical love and strength that can only be imagined by someone who doesn't possess those body parts that birthed a baby on a stable floor.

I wrap myself tighter in the thin hospital blanket. When I open my eyes again, sunlight is spilling out from underneath the drawn blinds. Mason is still dozing. I check his vitals on the monitor. I am surprised to have slept at all. But I'm so emptied out that there's space for a particular kind of grace that sneaks in when you're exhausted from guarding against everything else.

A few days later Dr. Fisher points to the circles on the tumor's white blur and says, "There are changes in the tumor that are new." Alan, Mason, and I stare at the computer screen. They've done another MRI. The changes look like Saturn rings, randomly drawn inside the tumor.

"This could be necrosis—the tumor cells dying—or it could be the tumor transforming into something else," he explains carefully. "We're recommending another biopsy. We're going to have to do something to treat this tumor, and we need to know exactly what we're dealing with."

"Great," Mason says with an irony that belies his eleven years. "Two brain surgeries."

Alan audibly exhales. I hold my breath. The plunge back into the deep end of uncertainty pushes me outside of feeling part of myself. There are no tears, only to-do lists.

## *thirteen*

# Magic Rice

A week after Mason's hospital stay, we're back as the neurosurgeon makes one small hole in Mason's head, then retrieves cells from several different sites in the tumor. When he wakes up, Mason responds well to the neurological tests.

"You're doing great, Mason," the nurse exclaims.

"Not bad for a kid who just had *brain surgery*," he says, leaning into his ominous horror-movie voice. His head is wrapped in gauze, and he smiles at his own joke.

Dr. Fisher reports, "It's good news. The tumor is a pilocytic astrocytoma. Pilocytic tumors don't change. It's always going to be low grade. It may become more aggressive; a grade one can still be a really nasty tumor."

It's a variation on Mason's original diagnosis in the same low grade, not necessarily predictable, family. There's a law of relativity in this new solar system of ours: good news isn't unqualified; there's a vortex of the unknown, unkind and unthinkable that is always gathering wind, threatening from just outside of now.

81

Dr. Fisher recommends a new drug therapy that targets the vascular system of tumors. The hope is that the drug will cut off the tumor's blood supply, which might shrink it, and reduce the likelihood of future bleeds. This biologic drug won't make Mason lose his hair. It won't cause nausea or immune deficiency because it targets the tumor with more specificity than typical chemo drugs. That's the good news.

The bad news is the drug, which will be administered in typical chemo fashion via infusion, might damage the kidneys, another vascular organ. To monitor that, they'll do urinalysis and frequent blood tests.

"But I want to lose my hair," Mason says.

He's trying to be funny.

"Mace . . ." Alan says, in a tired-daddy voice.

Mason is suffering and he wants people to know it. He still looks normal with his thick brown hair and bright green eyes, a few pimples emerging, like any other seventh grader. But he's not.

---

The reflexologist's office is a ratty-looking storefront, its windows opaque with grime. I circled the block for twenty minutes to find a parking spot that might minimize my children's exposure to gunfire or crack deals.

"Why do we all have to go?" Austin begged. "Why can't you just take us home?"

"If Mason wanted to go home, you'd take him," Sarah chimed in.

"Hey, I'm the one who has to have *chemotherapy*," Mason said.

I turned up the radio.

We heard about this reflexologist through an acquaintance who told us he'd cured a friend of a friend of pancreatic cancer using pressure point stimulation. Alan volunteered to try it himself and screen Rodney before we dragged Mason to one more appointment. He'd finished his treatment an hour before and insisted we come right away. Rodney agreed to fit us in.

I ring the doorbell of the office and wait for the *thunk* of the deadbolt's release.

Alan is waiting for us, looking out of place in his dark suit. He kisses my cheek as if a little affection could counteract the stress caused by crossing the Golden Gate Bridge on a Friday afternoon with three reluctant passengers under the age of fourteen.

The reflexology office is one big room fronted by a reception desk, empty except for a yellow legal pad with a handwritten instruction to "sign here." I add my name to the list along with Mason's, deciding I could use a relaxing foot massage too.

In the treatment area there are four reclining chairs upholstered in smoggy velour and covered with a patchwork of hand towels. At the foot of each chair there's a plastic tub. A young woman occupies the chair closest to us, resting her pale foot in Rodney's lap.

"Be with you in a minute." The white-haired man smiles.

Austin mouths, "How long is this going to take?"

Alan positions the children next to him on the sagging couch, anxiously awaiting Rodney's prognosis for Mason. As much as I can, I try to insulate Austin and Sarah by hiring babysitters who aren't emotionally devastated, shut down, or terrified like I've been in varying degrees since Mason's diagnosis. Nobody was available today on short notice. I understand Austin's frustration. I don't want to be here either.

Since the brain tumor revealed itself, everyone I know seems to know someone who puts me in six degrees of separation from a healing miracle. Before I wised up, my purse was filled with scraps of paper, names and numbers, connections to various sources of physical and psychic healing. Two years in, Mason has been to a chiropractic neurologist, two osteopaths, two herbalists, a nutritionist, two homeopaths, an acupuncturist, a Qigong master, and, of course, Christopher, the psychotherapist who does creative visualization. Total recovery is out there; it's just a matter of finding the expert—or the magic beans—that will make the tumor disappear as mysteriously as it arrived.

Good practitioners have helped calm Mason's headaches and even strengthened his immune system. But I've stopped taking referrals. It's too exhausting, repeating the story, juggling appointments, mounting the hope roller coaster again and again.

As if he's read my mind, Rodney offers me something tangible: "The best cup of tea in the world." He disappears through a curtain in the back of the room, then returns with a steaming cup. The lines around his dark eyes form a soft expression that I interpret as kindness.

"Ginseng tea from China. It will make you strong." Rodney hands me a Styrofoam cup half-filled with a rusty brown tea bag, a brew so bitter all I can do is pretend to sip. Then he motions for Mason to climb into a recliner and submerge his feet in a tub of warm water. I move into the recliner next to Mason's, slip off my sandals, and dip my feet into my own tub.

"The Lord gives us our own doctor—our feet," Rodney begins.

Mason smiles, sussing out Rodney.

Rodney pulls out an instrument that looks like a wooden handled corkscrew with a blunt end that he dips into a huge jar of Vaseline, then lifts Mason's dripping foot into the towel on his lap.

Alan watches, taking notes on his Blackberry and nodding.

"Such a good daddy you have. You are very lucky," Rodney says. He begins probing Mason's foot with his tool as he asks, "Does this hurt?"

Mason yelps.

Rodney nods sympathetically but continues doing what he's doing. "Come here, Mama, you need to feel this," he says. "It's his food; it's not good for him. Mama is responsible for his food."

I reach over and try to feel the indicator under Mason's toe, but it just feels like foot to me.

"He should only eat three things. Rice. Greens—no spinach.

Fruit—no mango. He doesn't need anything else. I sold special rice to your husband."

"We're very careful about what he eats," I assure him.

"Feel his feet. Not good." Rodney continues to shake his head.

"He doesn't eat junk food. He eats a lot of vegetables and fruit too."

"The feet do not lie," Rodney says, eyes sad for my poor child.

I'd forgotten my fairy tales. Just as the magic beans (or rice in Rodney's case) offer an improbable cure, if a child is hurting, he must have a careless mother who buys bad food and causes the suffering. I'm annoyed, but my psyche interprets this as good news. If I'm responsible, if I have that much power, then I can make it better. I'm not sure how, but I'll figure it out somehow. I envision myself as one of those mothers who could summon superhuman strength to lift a Chevy Suburban off of her child if need be. But this tumor is tricky because there is nowhere to grab on.

Rodney rubs Mason's feet with the towel and locks his eyes on him. "You need to come five times every week," he says.

"But I'm having surgery Monday morning."

"Why? No surgery. You come here."

I look up at Alan, hoping that the "good daddy" will support me, but his focus is on his Blackberry. He keeps typing with his thumbs, noting Rodney's recommendations.

I explain that Mason is having a port inserted in preparation for chemotherapy, that our neuro-oncologist suggested it was time to treat the tumor.

"Chemo is very bad," Rodney says. He tears a sheet off his pad and draws a male torso covered with mad black polka dots. "This man comes to me with cancer like this." Rodney grinds his pen into the dots for emphasis. "His mother wanted him to have chemo because she was afraid, but he was an adult and he said no. He came here instead. This boy has no choice. He is a child. He must do what you say."

"It's not the typical chemo drug," I protest defensively. "Our doctors are cautious and smart, really the very best."

"I will not see him if he gets chemo," Rodney says. "You must choose."

Untouched by the ultimatum he'd just delivered, he says, "Your turn."

I look to Alan, but he keeps thumbing his Blackberry in some sort of Ginseng tea–induced stupor.

"Another time," I say. "I need to feed these children."

"Come on, sweetie," Alan says. "Give it a try."

"Fifteen minutes, that's all," Rodney says.

Worn down by worry and low blood sugar, I put my feet into the old man's lap, feeling like the obstinate but ultimately obedient child I once was. Rodney digs his instrument into the Vaseline while I consider how much fungus can grow in a Costco-sized jar of petroleum jelly. I have a high tolerance for pain but when the probe sinks into my arch, the stab lifts my body off the chair.

"Your lymph system is vulnerable. You could get cancer. You could have cancer right now."

I don't believe him. I have to take care of my children, and Mason is starting chemo next week. I don't have time for cancer. Alan fingers his Blackberry, his face an impassive mask of a medical professional trained not to give away any feeling or doubt. Rodney and his torture instrument move a little farther up my arch. I choke back a scream.

"You are much too young to have such bad ovaries."

Tears stream down my face. Watching this from the couch across the room, my kids giggle nervously.

"Oh look, Mommy is a little chicken." Rodney smiles.

"Enough," I say. I point at Mason. "See that boy? I gave birth to him, a ten-pound baby, delivered in three hours without any drugs. I am no chicken."

Momentarily silenced, Rodney turns to the children. "Do not laugh at your mother. She is in pain."

I shoot Alan another scathing look.

"Just see what he has to say," Alan tells me. He's worried, not as convinced as I am of my invulnerability.

"Your husband is very smart. You are very fortunate," Rodney says.

Not feeling very fortunate, I push myself up from the chair, gather my purse, shoes, and children.

"Come back tomorrow. I have time for you both. Then come every day," Rodney shouts as the five of us hurry out the door.

"I'll call you," I lie. It's something I learned growing up, sneak out with an agreeable expression on your face, then run.

I belt the kids into the minivan, swallowing my rage and disappointment. I really do want to believe that there is a no-pain, no-side-effects treatment for my son. I want there to be "magic beans." As outraged as I am by Rodney, I am not quite ready to give up the search. In the meantime, I drive us to a place I know that serves the best gluten-free pizza, just this side of the Golden Gate Bridge. Anything but rice.

## fourteen

# Reality TV

It's Mason's first chemo appointment, and a phlebotomist named Bonnie accesses the port that was implanted last week, a small red gash in his otherwise unmarked chest. She fills three vials with blood, and he doesn't flinch.

The port, about the size of a quarter, is sealed by a soft top and connected to a catheter that accesses a vein near Mason's heart. It will be less painful than the search-and-poke method for starting an IV. Seeing the fresh wound on my son's chest is not painless for me. I put my head between my knees.

"Are you okay?" Bonnie asks.

"Yeah, I just forgot to look away. I've always been squeamish." *A good mother wouldn't look away from any of it*, I think.

When I describe Mason's treatment, I say, "We're getting chemo," or "We're getting a new biologic drug." But no one is piercing my skin. No one is taking blood from my veins.

We join my mom in the waiting room. A boy with a patch over one eye, about three years old, runs the length of the room. His mother chases him, and he laughs. She looks like she could use a nap. A little girl sits in front of the TV on a child-sized chair watching *Toy Story*. Her bright pink hat doesn't quite cover her bald head.

Mason reads *The Giver*, determined to finish his homework before he gets home so he can watch *Survivor* tonight. My mom flips through *O, The Oprah Magazine*. Silently I chant my mantra. *It's a different kind of chemo. Mason is not going to lose his hair. It won't make him sick.*

It doesn't help.

I try and fail to catch the eye of the young mom to let her know I get it. She's not alone. I flip through a copy of *InStyle* magazine, but don't find a feature on what to wear to your son's first chemo appointment, or recommendations for waterproof mascaras.

"I'm going to call Joan," I tell my mom. She offers a pained smile. I pace the bright lobby listening to my call ringing through to my friend's apartment in Sausalito.

"How's it going?" she asks.

"I'm sick. I forgot to look away when they took blood from Mason's port."

"It reminds you of your powerlessness," Joan says. "You're doing everything you can to fix this, and still there's so much you don't know. It's a lot. Breathe," Joan reminds me. "Right this minute, you're okay, and so is Mason."

I go back to the waiting room where I find Mason craning his neck to watch the movie. An attendant calls us, and we proceed to the next level, which means that Mason's (not my) blood counts are holding. We're escorted into the day hospital. Sun streams through the large picture window. Mason changes into the hospital gown while we wait behind the drawn curtain. I'm folding his clothes into a neat pile when the nurse enters.

"Hey, Mason, I'm Pearl. I'll be taking care of you today."

Pearl is tiny, with thick brown hair and bright brown eyes. She attaches Mason to the monitors, peeling stickers off the leads and sticking them to his chest. His heart rate and oxygen saturation levels appear on the screen next to the bed.

"And how are you today?" Mason asks in the gentlemanly tone of a much older person.

"I'm doing well," Pearl answers. "How about you?"

"Just terrific for a kid getting chemo," he says. "At least we brought doughnuts."

Pearl laughs. "I see. Doughnuts are part of your chemo protocol. Sounds good to me," she says as she hangs a small plastic bag of medication from the IV pole. It appears so innocuous: clear, clean liquid dripping one drop at a time into the port next to Mason's heart.

"Mason, do you have the remote?" Mom asks as she opens the box of doughnuts.

Mason flips through the channels and settles on *Wife Swap*, a reality show on which families trade moms for a week to get some perspective on how good they have it. A mother of two is packing her suitcase, hoping to teach her swap family the value of structure and football. Mason twists to reach for a second cinnamon sugar doughnut, and the alarm goes off in the IV pump. Manic, worried beeps fill the room. Pearl returns and calmly massages the kinked line between her thumb and index finger, restoring the flow.

"There you go," Pearl says. "How are those doughnuts?"

"Gooood," Mason says. "Do you want one? They're gluten-free."

"Not right now," Pearl says, then smiles. "But thanks."

The sugar-free rule has been revoked. I figure that if Mason eats his fill of vegetables and protein, a little sugar isn't going to hurt. Mostly I'm too worn out to fight. But it turns out gluten really does give him (and me) brutal headaches, so it's even more fun when we find unexpected treats like these doughnuts.

"So, Mason," I say, "what kind of mom would they swap me for?"

He answers without hesitation. "Someone who eats fast food every night and hates all animals except the hairless ones."

The three of us laugh.

The show makes me feel like an excellent mother and a generally sane person, which seems to be the point of reality TV. At least I'm not that bad.

As the medication flows steadily into my son's chest, we laugh again, and it feels good and genuine. I text Alan. He's at a can't-miss-meeting in New York, feeling guilty about not being here. I reassure him it's all good.

After two hours Pearl returns and unhooks the empty bag. "Looks like you get to go home now," she says. "How are you feeling?"

"No complaints," Mason says in his half-joking, old-man tone. He's smiling, ready to be done. I hand him his clothes.

Outside the hospital I hug my mom goodbye. "Thanks for being here," I say. We maintain our cheerful, we-won't-let-this-tumor-get-us-down attitude. Either she holds me a little longer, or I don't pull away as quickly as I usually do.

Mason and I climb into the car. "One down," I say, and hand him a water bottle.

"Yay," he answers in his ironic voice.

I'm happy to be headed home. But as I watch the other moms on the road speeding past me to pick up carpools, to ferry kids to tutors, play dates, and soccer practice, I realize I don't belong in the world of mothers who worry about test scores and too much screen time.

I am still living in that world. There's an e-mail from Sarah's tutor, who recommends that we up her weekly sessions to two. Austin wants me to proofread his paper on *Macbeth*. But something has shifted. I might look the same, but I'm not. A cache of knowledge has opened up to me though I'm not fluent in its language yet. It's a shift of perspective that comes from sitting in a room with three children waiting for chemotherapy. How can I worry about Austin's English grade when Mason's kidneys might be under siege? I can and I do, but maybe not as much.

When I wake up the next morning, fog rests on the hillside outside my kitchen window. I pull on a down jacket and walk to the end of the driveway to get the newspaper. We've been back in our real house a few months now, and the garden makes me smile every morning. The rhododendrons bloom plump red flowers. The leaves of the mock-orange tree are fluorescent against the gray sky.

My neighbor Angela is walking her sheepdog Harley. I want to pretend that I don't see her, but that would be rude, so I wave.

"How's Mason?" Her voice takes on that low, sad tone people use with us these days.

"We started chemo yesterday," I say as Harley noses the cuffs of my pajama pants. "He's doing well," I add. "He's getting a new drug that won't make him sick and won't make his hair fall out."

"I would never do chemo," Angela says smartly. "Why poison the whole body? Radiation makes so much more sense to me. It's targeted."

Her overwhelming confidence lands like a tight-fisted punch. Or is it arrogance? Too stunned to rage, though the feeling registers, I forget that I have the right to remain silent.

"It's not that kind of chemo," I sputter, wishing I'd never opened the gate, resisting the urge to run up to the house and retrieve the tape-recorded conversations with our doctors, evidence that we made the right decisions, that I'm a good mother, making smart choices. "This drug targets the vascularity of his tumor," I explain, proving that we've looked under every rock, that we've gotten second, third, and even fourth opinions. I don't know why I care what Angela thinks, but I'm overpowered by my need to convince her that, thanks to our diligence, Mason's getting the best treatment possible.

"But what are the long-term side effects? It's like a time bomb," Angela insists.

My confidence hemorrhages out of me. My worry about Mason overrides my cellular-level loathing of Angela in this moment. Did we jump into chemotherapy too soon? Will the treatment kill my son, even if the tumor doesn't?

I've spent my whole life wanting people to validate me, to see me as smart, capable, and *right*. I know it comes from growing up as I did, needing to be so good and above reproach so that my father wouldn't look in my direction when he needed someone to blame for how miserable he felt drunk or hungover. But self-knowledge isn't a cure-all, and I feel an awkward, unwelcome vulnerability standing here in my pajama pants.

I don't explain to Angela why the Tumor Board ruled out radiation right now. I don't mention Mason's bleed or the size of the tumor. I hug the newspaper to my chest.

Luckily Harley pulls Angela to a better smell up the hill.

"Let me know if you need groceries or anything . . . call me," she shouts over her shoulder.

Shaken and pissed off, I call Annie instead.

"Can you believe she had the nerve to ask me what the long-term side effects are?"

"Life!" Annie answers, and we laugh.

Angela can afford to be self-righteous. She has the luxury of forming opinions without actual experience. I miss that delicious feeling of rightness, the illusion that I can outsmart actual suffering, maybe even death, with the superior power of my mind. As this nightmare has unfolded, that kind of certainty was one of the first things to go. Like a frostbitten toe, it isn't growing back. I'm learning to balance without it.

## fifteen

# Dust into Clay

Weeks pass—one blood draw, one infusion, one dozen gluten-free doughnuts at a time. There's no time to feel what I fear is looming just beyond my line of sight. Alan and I pray together when we're in the same city, sometimes over the phone too. Our marriage has taken on an Olympic-relay quality. Romance has been mostly replaced with appreciation. But I do feel sincere gratitude when Alan takes Mason to chemo, when he picks up takeout on his way home from the airport, when our gold-standard health insurance sends us another statement outlining medical bills paid. I don't think about the closeness I'm not feeling right now because this would be disloyal, not just to my husband but to our present circumstances, our family. We push through, side by side or alone; we do what has to be done.

Tumor or no tumor, everyone is growing up. Austin, fifteen, is a freshman in high school. He's out every weekend with his best friend, Sam, in pursuit of that illusive destination where the fun is happening in our sleepy county. On one of these Saturday nights, Alan and I are driving home from a rare dinner out with friends when Austin calls.

95

"Can I spend the night at Ryan's dad's house?" Austin asks us over Bluetooth.

"Why don't you spend the night at Sam's instead?" I say, locking eyes with Alan who looks as suspicious as I feel. I don't know Ryan's father, but there's a reason the kids always want to hang out at his house.

"You guys don't trust me," Austin says.

He's right, of course.

"Why don't you stay at Ryan's mom's house?" I ask. We picked him up there a few weeks ago, and she seemed sane, nice.

"She's in Europe with her boyfriend," Austin explains, like *duh*.

"We'll call you back," Alan says, ending the call.

"They're at the mom's house right now," he says.

Alan drives to Ryan's mom's house. I wait in the car while Alan walks toward the door. He doesn't get far because there are no curtains and the party is framed by a huge picture window.

"I don't see Austin, but the kids in there are getting high," he calls over to me, startled, shaking his head. We've stumbled into one of those parenting moments you read about in books. Austin appears down the street, walking toward the house with Sam. The expression on his face is relaxed, happy. When he sees us, a look of horror transforms him.

"What the hell?" Austin sputters.

"Get in the car," Alan yells. *"Now!"*

There's some resistance but he succumbs, climbing into the back seat where he moans, "You're ruining my life."

I don't want to ruin his life, but I'll do what I have to do. We negotiate a peace settlement over the next few days: Austin won't lie, he'll tell us where he is, and we'll start believing him most of the time. I continue to hold my breath on Friday and Saturday nights. I buy three more Blessed Mary scapulars at the Mission store and secretly distribute them under everyone's mattresses. The logical part of me knows that God either is or isn't. That a loving, all-powerful source won't necessarily bestow extra blessing for a three-dollar, mass-produced necklace with a stamped image of Mary. But it's something I can do. An intention. A plea. And maybe enough desperate pleas will accumulate like dust into clay, forming a fortification.

Finally, finally: Mason's last infusion. In his chemo room, a thin teen-age boy sits tall in the next bed. He's pale, with dusty blue eyes he got from his mother who blinks at us, adjusting her gaze from the computer in her lap.

"Hi," Mason says as he climbs onto his own bed. "I'm Mason."

"I'm Mitch."

I smile at Mitch, and so does my mom. Mitch's mother smiles back. There are no walls, no physical barriers dividing us, only a cur-tain that we draw so Mason can change into a gown. I attempt to master hospital etiquette—when to look at a fellow patient or his par-ent and when to look away, when to reach out, when to retreat into respectful silence. I've gotten better at avoiding the reflexive question "How are you?" when I know the answer will be complicated.

Mitch hacks loudly and clears his throat. I hear him spit into a bedpan.

"Hi, Mason." Pearl enters with the bag of medication.

"It's my last chemo," Mason tells her with a grin.

"You should have a party," she says, hanging the bag on the pole next to his bed.

"Yeah, but it might be weird. People would say, 'Yay, your brain tumor is gone.' And I'd be all, "Uh, no, it's actually not,'" Mason considers.

Therein lies our dilemma, or rather, our new way of life. The tumor is enmeshed in Mason's brain, so it isn't going anywhere. The best we can hope for is to disable it so it doesn't grow and it doesn't bleed. Months have passed since the first IV bag of medication emptied into the shunt in Mason's chest. The port is now a small dash of a scar. Mason has had no visible adverse reaction. He hasn't gotten sick. His hair is messy and thick.

On our way in this morning, when the medical assistant, Candido, asked Mason to stand against the measuring stick on the wall, he proclaimed, "You're five feet, eleven inches. How old are you again?"

"I'm twelve and I'm taller than my older brother." Mason did a happy dance. Candido laughed.

"That drug," I said, "works as well as Miracle-Gro."

Mason stretches out in the hospital bed, his feet pushing against the plastic footboard. As he's done each time before, Mason clicks the remote and turns on *Wife Swap*. He bites into one of the powdered sugar doughnuts we brought, unleashing a dusting of white around his nose.

Dr. Fisher's nurse practitioner comes into the room. Trish has chestnut hair and matching glasses that frame her smart eyes. She and Mason exchange high fives.

"How's your last chemo going?" she asks with genuine cheer.

"Well, I won't be able to use chemo as an excuse anymore." Mason grins. "But I can still say I have brain cancer."

"You're still getting away with that one?" Trish says.

We all laugh. Then Trish does a quick neuro check, finger to nose, follow my finger with your eyes, check pupils for even dilation. Mason scores well.

"If I don't see you before you leave, congratulations," she says. "I'll see you when you come for your MRI."

As Trish leaves, a friend comes to visit Mitch. It's impossible not to eavesdrop on the two teenage boys. "I'm in no shape to have a bone marrow transplant now, but this chemo will give me some time,"

Mitch is saying. "If the cancer comes back, it'll be in two or three years. Then I'll be strong enough to handle it."

"Sounds good," his friend answers.

*Mason has a different kind of cancer*, I remind myself. *It's hardly cancer at all.* I ask God to help Mitch and his mother, and us.

Today's episode of *Wife Swap* features a woman from Iowa who's a raw foodie, but not the kind you find in our neck of the Marin woods, where devotees grind carrots, almonds, and zucchini together to make "meat" loaf. These people eat real beef uncooked, like we've all been taught not to do.

"Ewww," Mason groans as the swapped mom opens the refrigerator in the raw people's kitchen. My mom laughs. She has a powdered sugar mustache too. I slip out of the room and find Trish at the nurse's station.

"I know you already told me this," I say, "but when will we know if the chemo worked?"

"If we're lucky, we'll see some improvement on the next scan in eight weeks. But it could take some time." She peers at me. "How are you doing?"

"I'm okay. Happy to have made it through without any major problems."

"Mason's a champ," Trish says. "You know, finishing treatment is often harder on parents than they think it's going to be. It sounds counterintuitive, but you've been taking aggressive action against the tumor. Now you just have to wait and see what happens."

"I hadn't thought of that," I say, "but it explains a lot." I've been feeling panicked lately at odd times. I'd dismissed one possible reason after another. Yes, my son is finishing chemo. Yes, my husband is in an intense push at work that requires him to travel five days out of each week. Yes, I have two other children with needs. But the anxiety has felt outsized, a paralyzing contraction of looming doom. It takes me by surprise every time.

"It's really hard," Trish says with a warm hand on my shoulder. I want to crawl into her lap and sob like a baby. Instead, I sniff and rub away tears before they collect in the corners of my eyes. *This is a happy day*, I remind myself. I want to feel relieved.

# sixteen

# Purgatory

Rascal's still alive," Sarah says. She's on her knees in the hall closet where our eighteen-year-old dying cat is hiding. He's invisible, a black cat in a dark closet, until he opens his yellow eyes. We're three days into hospice mode, checking his breathing, using a syringe to squirt kitty morphine between his black leather lips.

My sadness is stuck below layers of fear about Mason. After his last scan, the Tumor Board declared the tumor stable, which technically means unchanged for better or worse. But when we looked at the scans with Dr. Fisher, Alan pointed to a white whirl with a hollow gray center about a half-centimeter around: one of the rings we'd been watching for months now.

"Isn't that bigger than it was before?" Alan asked. I wanted to tell him that the Tumor Board didn't need a freelance consult. I wanted to take our "stable" diagnosis and run for the door. But I stayed silent, in a lips-pressed-together way. The last thing I needed was an argument with Alan in front of Dr. Fisher.

"It could mean a few things," Dr. Fisher said. "It could mean the tumor is becoming more active. It could be necrosis, the tumor breaking down."

As the one in charge of keeping the glass half full, I asked a suitably feel-good question. "Wouldn't that be a good thing, that the tumor is breaking down? Maybe even dying?"

"That's one possibility," Dr. Fisher replied carefully.

Therein lies the sucky-ness, the purgatory of living with a child who's living with a tumor. Even the "good" news is couched in disclaimers. We remain in a state of "wait and see." Mason hasn't had a bleed since the chemo. He's managing to get mostly *A*s in school, marking up *To Kill a Mockingbird* with Post-its and highlighter pens in a messy sort of brilliance. He's thinking about trying out for the rowing team.

---

Rascal's imminent passing shakes me. Yes, I'll miss my cat, but the underlying reason is dire. I'm afraid my marriage will fall apart without him. That sounds unreasonable, even in my state of grief and sleep deprivation. But Alan and I chose Rascal the summer before we got married, when we loved each other without hesitation or aggravation. Now we're entering some sort of foggy, cold, post-Rascal stage, and I'm not sure what will happen to us.

There are two adolescent kittens sleeping on a cat tree near the kitchen door: Cowboy is black with ears too big for his thin, triangular face. Tulip is a tortoiseshell, a longhaired palette of rust, black, and white. We adopted the two of them in a moment of extreme optimism, when emotional exhaustion blocked more rational thoughts, like *I will be stuck with these two animals for the next eighteen years*. Now I know not to trust the impulse to "stop by" the Humane Society in the midst of a medical crisis or possibly ever.

"How much extra work could two kittens be?" Alan had asked as we watched them play together in their cage. The answer was absolutely none, especially when your wife is taking care of the kittens and everything else while you're sleeping at a nice hotel in Manhattan.

I love Alan because he couldn't leave the little black kitten meowing alone. For the same reason, Alan is as troubled by his inability to make me happy these days as he is by his own unhappiness. He was an Eagle Scout, my husband. He wants to help. But no matter how many hours he works, no matter how much cash he deposits in our accounts, no matter how many "good" questions he asks of the doctors, he can't guarantee that we're going to be okay. He can't fix what's wrong with our family because it's not fixable.

We say "I love you" nearly every day. But there is subterranean movement in our relationship, something that might show up as whirls on a scan. I'm afraid of the distance between us, the disagreements, the frustrations. As married people do, we continue the march of our relationship out of muscle memory, out of commitment, out of a longing for a closeness that we don't happen to be feeling right now.

This includes a weekly date, Sunday lunch, just the two of us at our favorite restaurant. We could walk there if Alan's knees weren't still bothering him from a mountain bike mishap a few months ago. Alan takes an extreme approach to everything he does, unlike me, who rides her bike with the ever-present thought of how an injury might derail the family carpool system and intricate web of appointments.

I cool my hands on my sweating glass of iced tea with mango. "You can tell everything you need to know about a restaurant by its iced tea," I say. "If they bother to get the iced tea right, you can bet they know what they're doing with the food."

Alan laughs. I like that he still laughs at my silly observations. I smile at him as the waiter brings our salads, two big bowls of romaine with slices of chicken breast, olives, and feta cheese.

"I'm trying to get my calendar figured out for the next couple of months," Alan says. "I have a conference in Brussels the week of your birthday, but I booked a flight home for the weekend. I was wondering if you'd meet me in New York. We haven't been to New York together in a long time."

"I can see if my mom can stay with the kids. But we don't really know what's going to be happening with Mason."

Being on duty with Mason is too much to ask a babysitter, almost too much to ask a grandparent. We're on 24-7 tumor watch. It's not something you can request a leave of absence from. I don't want to say no to my husband, but I'm not sure I can say yes.

I do such a good job of taking care of everything, Alan can be oblivious to the work required. Then again, I wonder if Alan finds it painful to look too closely at what it takes to live in uncertain peace with an unpredictable tumor. There are the headaches ("What number is it, Mace? Are you nauseated? Did you finish your water?"), the exhaustion (some nights Mason's in bed by seven), and the chronic watch for the next reason to rush to the ER. Then there's Sarah who, at age ten, has taken to falling asleep in my arms again. And Austin who, at fifteen, is the age I was when I found my savior in a bottle of Bacardi rum.

"Say yes," he says. "It'll be fun."

Fun? It seems like a ridiculous concept, an extravagance like a two-seated Porsche 911 or a $50,000 Birkin bag. I buy my purses on Kate Spade's clearance, waiting for the double markdowns. I drive a minivan with a five-star safety rating.

I wave to the waiter for a refill, chiding myself for my bad attitude. I should appreciate my husband for wanting to spend time with me. I should want to spend time with him. And I do. I gauge my love for my husband in the uptick I feel when I answer the phone and he's on the other end. I figure that some woman ten years younger than I am, with a much more agreeable disposition and a less complicated life, would find him fabulous. This is the cautionary tale I tell myself. I know better than ever that marriage, like cancer and child-rearing, is an endurance sport. The point of the contract is to hang on through the thin, brittle places when it's commitment, not passion or even friendship, that carries the relationship from one day to the next.

Alan's new wife, I warn myself in my darker moments, would think that life with Alan was one big vacation: all those conference invitations with spouses included (the invitations I ignore), the dinners at fancy restaurants dressed in nice clothes.

I'm also annoyed. Alan is inviting me to join him as if I can just blink—as he does—and have the children cared for, the house maintained, and the healthy dinners prepared. What if I go and something happens while I'm away?

The cat tried to follow his animal instinct to die alone. A few days ago he pushed past me out the kitchen door, each step deliberate, conserving his limited energy. I followed him to the corner of our lot, where I found a raccoon-sized hole in the fence. He lifted his eyes to the grassy hillside dotted with bay trees, clumps of poison oak and blackberry, but I picked him up and carried him inside before he could step into the gap. There are coyotes and dogs and hawks out there. I would never let him die that way.

Alan thought I should have let him go. It's easy to say this by phone from a high-rise office building in San Francisco where people are lined up outside your door to talk to you about investment strategies, and you're dealing with clean, dispassionate numbers—not the final transformation of a beloved creature from muscle and bone to dust. Tonight I make a washable, towel-and-plastic-bag nest for

Rascal in my bed, and I doze off with my arm around him. Tomorrow morning, I will take him to the vet so she can release him from his crumbling body. For now, I hold a warm hand over his heart.

When Alan comes home at ten p.m., he kisses me on the forehead, strokes the cat, then retreats downstairs by himself, answering e-mails late into the night.

*seventeen*

# Floods and Mudslides

I meet Annie at Starbucks, something we rarely do. We have too many conversations for each one to merit a table and coffee, but this morning Annie insists. We claim two window seats while the playlist humming from hidden speakers helps us pretend that the red-haired man at the next table isn't overhearing our entire conversation.

"Mason's been having a lot of headaches," I say, reflexively checking my phone for missed calls. "But he still wants to go to school every day."

Eight weeks ago, Mason had a surgery to insert a shunt in his brain to help drain the cerebral fluid that had become dammed up by his tumor. It was a quick stay in the hospital, and it was supposed to alleviate the headaches. It helped for a little while.

Annie's face softens into a compassionate sigh.

"Dr. Fisher suggested that we meet with the radiation oncologist, just in case we need her at some point. No one knows for sure what the changes in the tumor mean. It could be good news—the tumor breaking down."

I present my case logically, but my optimism is as tired as the rest of me. The red-haired man at the next table glances over his shoulder, pretending to check the length of the line for refills.

Annie picks up my iced-tea cup, the wrapper from my dried apple snack, and her coffee cup and arranges them equidistant before me. This seems to be the moment she's been waiting for, the reason she called this meeting.

"This is your emotional acre," she says. "Everyone has one—me, you, Mason. Growing up in alcoholism, people like us thought we'd be safe if only we could control everything on our acre and everybody else's. If we could get the outside to shine, we had a chance. We might be okay."

This is an idea some friends had been talking about lately, as in staying on their own emotional acres, not trespassing on their partner's or children's grassy areas. It's a pastoral image for minding one's own business, which presumes there's a tender place inside each of us where we hold this life of ours and try to make sense of it.

"Here's everything Mason has going for him: he's smart."

She moves the snack bag wrapper to the center of the table, a marker on the tabletop which has apparently become the game board symbolizing my complicated emotional life, the one I attempt to push into a leak-proof, ziplock bag inside myself, so it doesn't drown me.

"He's strong."

She moves the paper cup next to the wrapper—smart and strong, side by side.

"Here is the part of the acre you're not allowed to talk about. The part with the brambles, the scary part, because it seems like it would be disloyal for you to go there."

Amber-colored tea sloshes over the melting ice cubes in my Venti cup—the "he who must not be named" part of my acre, my life.

"You need to be able to say what's most scary about this. The things we try to push away get more powerful."

The unspeakable: I am afraid the tumor will consume Mason. It's his brain, for God's sake, that part of him that makes him who he is. I'm afraid of losing him.

I don't say this out loud, and neither does Annie.

I drive home with tears streaming down my face. I'm like the little Dutch boy in the children's story with his finger in the dam. I've persuaded myself that I have the power to tilt the story toward the miracle, the only acceptable conclusion, because the alternative acknowledges the tidal wave on the other side of the floodgates.

Something's wrong with Mason. Really wrong. He's had headaches nearly every day for two weeks. Bad headaches that send him to bed with a dose of Vicodin, no television, no dessert. Trish schedules an emergency MRI, and we're back in Dr. Fisher's office with the MRI scans on his computer screen.

"There's an area of new growth in the tumor." Dr. Fisher's voice is practiced and even. "Our greatest worry is a massive bleed, one that won't be so easy for Mason to recover from."

This is what the chemo was supposed to prevent. I feel sick. Alan stares at the screen. Mason is uncharacteristically quiet, frozen. Dr. Fisher clicks through the images one by one. I see a white shadow superimposed on the tumor, a spot the size of a pea protruding where it wasn't before.

Mason sits up on the table and leans toward the screen. There are no jokes, no tears. Not yet.

"The Tumor Board met to review all of our options. Weighing risks and benefits, we agreed that at this point, it's best to pursue a surgical solution."

"But—," I start, then stop myself.

"Dr. Edwards believes he can de-bulk the tumor. He won't resect the whole thing, that would be too dangerous to Mason's brain, but he can remove enough to make a difference."

Suddenly the brain surgery that was our worst-case scenario is now our best option. My vision blurs with tears. Alan reaches for Mason's hand, and for mine.

Back in the car Alan cuts off a minivan merging onto the freeway. Mason stares out the window. I'd like to remember to have compassion for distracted drivers, who might be people like us, sent home with life-altering news. There should be a car service, an undisturbed professional in a well-marked vehicle, that would let others know to give you a wide berth.

"Crap," Mason says.

"That about sums it up," I answer.

"Damn it," Alan mutters, passing a Volvo. I don't know why we're in such a hurry to get home, but this time, I don't scold Alan. I don't have the energy. I'm leaking tears, summoning everything in me not to break down, not to make Mason more scared than he already is.

"Thank goodness you have such good doctors," I say. "People come from all over the world to have Dr. Edwards operate on their kids. He's that good." My voice quavers.

"It's easy for you to say that," Mason says. "Nobody's going to drill a hole in *your* head."

⸺

When we get home, Sarah and Austin are doing their homework in the kitchen. They immediately know something's up. The air around us is heavy and ominous, like the palpable stillness before an earthquake. Mason walks past them and upstairs to his room. There's no quip about brain cancer, no mention of missing school while his brother and sister are stuck doing their work.

"What's up with him?" Austin asks.

"The tumor grew," I say. "Mason is going to have surgery. They'll take out what they can."

"That sucks," he says, eyes focusing on a sheet of graph paper in front of him. I can see Austin's mind shifting, taking this in. At sixteen, he's memorized the formula of implications as if it's an algebra proof. He blinks back tears. Alan squats down and pulls him into a sideways hug.

"When?" Sarah asks, her voice panicky. I sit down next to her and she climbs into my lap. She needs to know what to expect. What to plan for.

"Soon," Alan says. "We're meeting with the brain surgeon the day after tomorrow."

I heat up a leftover pasta that I don't eat. I pour kibble in the dogs' bowls. I sort the laundry. Alan cancels two business trips. We hold each other after the kids go to sleep. We recite a prayer we've said together many times, grateful for the well-worn groove of the words. Alan falls asleep, but I don't even try. I open my notebook. The only way to get through the unimaginable is to fill in the squares on the calendar, to make a list, and check it off. It's forward motion: inadequate, and the only thing I can do.

Two days later we meet with the neurosurgeon and choose a date. Pre-surgery, Mason will be checked into the hospital where the team will map his brain, identifying areas critical to speech, movement, and senses. Mason's remarkable ability to function is testament to his brain's success in relocating vital functions. The surgeons will do everything they can to minimize damage by avoiding these areas. It's science fiction, a blessing thrown in with whatever this experience is.

I pray, grudgingly. The scariest thought is that I'm as alone as I feel. Maybe the aloneness comes from knowing that no one, even my devoted friends and tireless family, can make it better. There's a hollowness inside. My prayer is the wind in this empty place where I am not able to form words. I mostly register terror along with a healthy

THE OPPOSITE OF CERTAINTY

indignation regarding God's *supposed* plan. But I keep these thoughts to myself, because *Are you kidding me?* is not necessarily a prayer that will get results.

Annie tells me that I need to get the anger out, which feels like an accusation. What anger? Sadness I'd cop to, obviously, but anger?

To me, anger is like demonic possession, dangerous and unpredictable. My grandpa woke up most Sunday mornings with an empty quart of bourbon he didn't remember buying and remorse enough to fill the fist-shaped holes in the walls. I was ten when I realized that the scar on my beloved grandma's nose matched the shape of the ring my grandfather wore on his right hand.

Losing control terrifies me.

I prefer blame, because underneath it there's the illusion of change, movement, and control. If I can figure out what or who went wrong, then maybe I can force them to change so that things will be okay. It's terrifying, this lava pit in the middle of me, the mix of rage, fear, and bewilderment. If I'm not the grateful good girl, will the Powers That Be toss my son off this precarious planet?

Maybe I do need to let this out.

The next day, driving home from the store with my good-mama bags of cruciferous vegetables, chewable vitamin D, and grass-fed, omega 3-rich, organic hamburger, I wait until the traffic on Third Street is moving at a decent clip so no one is next to me, and I scream.

My first attempt is weak, a sick lion's roar. Joan would say it's because I'm not breathing. I'm in my head. I speed up to pass a Volkswagen and try again.

*"Aaaahhhh!"*

This time I feel it in my throat. Encouraged, I try again. By the time I turn onto our street, the inside of my throat feels stretched and raw. My emotional acre? It's scorched and vulnerable to floods and mudslides.

*eighteen*

## Precarious

The day before our neurosurgery pre-op appointment, Mason comes home from school with another headache. I give him a Vicodin and tuck him in on the couch with a big glass of water and the TV remote.

I put some chicken breasts into the oven, along with miniature potatoes that I toss with garlic and olive oil.

"Are you okay?" I call out to Mason.

"Yeah," he says, but his voice is wrung out, pain-infused. He's crawling through one injurious moment to the next. There is nothing I can do for him.

I put a plate of crackers on the table next to the couch along with another glass of water. Mason is watching TV, *Seinfeld* again, his head propped up on pillows, the lights dim. He laughs out loud. I hear him get up and open the door for the dog. All good. Back in the kitchen, I cut the stems off a bunch of broccoli, spray the tiny blooms with water, and chop them into fork-friendly pieces. Austin is at Sam's house. It's quiet except for the dog snoring in a puddle of receding sunlight.

Alan is home for dinner. Mason manages a few bites before retreating back to the couch.

"Anyone want to get ice cream?" Alan asks.

"Yes!" Sarah answers quickly.

"Mason?"

"I don't feel like it," he says. This is most telling, most sad. Eighteen hours until our appointment with Dr. Edwards, thank God.

"We'll stay here," I say. "Go ahead."

I dump a load of clean laundry on the couch. Mason flips through the list of shows on the DVR.

"I feel sick," he says.

I grab a bucket from the laundry room and put it next to him. I stroke his back, and he seems a little better after this. I hold up a glass of water for him to sip and offer him another pill. Then I finish folding and stacking the clothes into neat piles.

Not being able to do anything about my child's pain, I feel hopeless, helpless, and a failure. But at least we know what's causing the headaches. At least the team is on it. Mason laughs again as I go into the bathroom and stack towels on a shelf.

"How are you doing?" I call.

"Okay," he says in a weak voice.

I load the dishwasher. I can't sit still, but luckily there is plenty to do. Alan and Sarah return, and Sarah jogs up the stairs to her room.

That's when Alan calls out, "Something's wrong."

"I know," I say exasperated. This is my job. "He's been having these headaches for weeks now," I say in an angry whisper. "We're seeing Dr. Edwards at eleven tomorrow."

But at this moment the headache morphs into something else, something much worse.

"It's really bad," Mason moans. He's rocking, head in hands.

Alan and I exchange a terrified look. It's what we've been warned about. We both know without speaking it aloud. I put my arm around

Mason. I stroke his back and his shoulders as Alan dials Dr. Fisher's cell phone. He paces, head down, a hand over the ear that's not against the phone.

"Yes, she gave him Vicodin," he tells Dr. Fisher. "He's conscious. The pain got so bad, all of a sudden. It's getting worse. . . . Okay, I'll call you."

Alan hangs up and grabs his keys off the windowsill. I walk Mason to the door. He leans on me.

"Dr. Fisher says it's probably a bleed," Alan says. "He's having dinner with Edwards. They're calling Trish. She's getting the team ready. We need to take him to Marin General and get him seen right away, then get him down to Stanford as soon as we can."

Alan takes Mason from me and they step out the door. Mason is in socks. He rests his head on Alan's shoulder.

I follow behind them. The stone patio is cold under my bare feet.

"I'll be right behind you."

My mind skids and stops. My purse. The insurance card. Tell Sarah what's happening. Hold her. Call Austin, Dad, Mom. "It's an emergency," I say. "A bleed."

---

Alan waits outside an ER cubicle, talking to Dr. Fisher on his phone. Inside, a team of nurses in green scrubs connects wires and tubes to Mason. An oxygen mask is covering his mouth and nose.

"I'm here," I say, edging past the blonde nurse to stroke Mason's shoulder. His eyes are closed, as if he's napping. He doesn't respond to the bevy of nurses around him. His leg shakes, and I put a hand on his thigh to steady it.

A doctor introduces himself as Dr. Ruben and summons a couple of orderlies. Mason is rushed to an emergency CT scan. In minutes we have results.

"We've confirmed that there's been a hemorrhage," the doctor says. "There's a lot of blood escaping into his brain. We need to insert a drain into your son's skull immediately to reduce the pressure. We don't have a neurosurgeon on duty, so Mason needs to be transported to Stanford."

"Trish is ordering a helicopter to pick him up," Alan says.

"I'll confirm the logistics for the transfer," Dr. Ruben replies.

He's back three minutes later. Mason is blessedly unconscious, not appearing to be in pain.

"The helicopter is grounded because of fog," he says. "I've called in the neurosurgeon we have on call tonight. He's on his way."

I am drowning, suffocating. I can't catch my breath.

"Where's he coming from?" Alan asks. His eyes are frantic, desperate.

"He lives in San Francisco," Dr. Ruben answers with a calm that belies this bad news. Depending on where the neurosurgeon lives in the city, it might be thirty to forty minutes before he can drill a hole in Mason's head to stabilize him.

My fingers tremble on the white sheet that is pulled up to Mason's chest. I would insert the drain myself if I could. My hands are empty and inadequate.

"We need to intubate him to protect his airway," Dr. Ruben says. "It would be best if you step outside while we do this."

Dr. Ruben pulls the thin cotton curtain closed. Alan and I wait on the other side in a well-traveled hallway. We try not to block the way of the doctors and nurses who pass by. It's a busy night.

Alan puts his arms around me. I fold myself into his body. My head rests over his heart, the way it always has.

"God," Alan begins to pray, "I offer myself to You to build with me and do with me as You will . . ."

It is an old prayer we've said together many times, including at the altar at our wedding, about having a higher purpose, aspiring to do God's will in this world, which assumes that God's will is a good thing. I can't speak the words tonight, because at the moment I'm not sure this is true.

"Take away my difficulties, that victory over them may bear witness to those I would help of Thy power, Thy love, and Thy way of life," Alan continues.

I press my face against his chest, hiding my silence. I've had enough of God "doing with me." I don't aspire to strength or spiritual fortitude. I just want my boy to be okay. My unsaid prayer is, "Knock it *off*."

Alan and I pull apart, distracted by the automatic doors opening and closing. An unconscious woman in her fifties is rolled in on a gurney by paramedics; another family assumes its vigil alongside her bed. I text Austin and Sarah asking them to pack some clothes, contact lens solution, my glasses.

Two cubicles down, a thin man with gray hair that matches the color of his skin attempts to walk out of his curtained cubicle in his backless hospital gown. He curses drunkenly when the tether of his IV pole pulls him back inside.

We watch the clock, every second in ER time stretched by our knowledge that Mason's brain is inflating like a water balloon. We need a neurosurgeon now, not ten minutes from now.

A middle-aged man appears in front of us in wrinkled navy slacks and a rumpled shirt.

"I'm the neurosurgeon who will be performing the procedure on your son." He beckons us to a computer monitor with Mason's scan on the screen. It looks like India ink has been poured over the white blur of the tumor.

"We'll put in a temporary drain to relieve the pressure. This should stabilize him so you can transport him to Stanford. It's a quick procedure, maybe fifteen minutes, that we do at the bedside."

Alan and I resume our waiting position outside of Mason's

curtained cubicle, holding hands. Raw fear beats out my frustration with Whomever is pulling the strings in this universe.

I repeat the prayer, *Help. Please. Help.*

Alan texts Dr. Fisher an update. I text my mom, who's already waiting for us at Stanford, and my dad who's on his way to stay with the kids. I text Annie and Joan.

Ten minutes later, a blonde nurse pulls open the curtain for us.

"It went well," the neurosurgeon says. "The pressure is relieved. He's stable, and you can move him."

"Thank you," Alan says.

"Thank you," I say, with gratitude beyond any I've ever felt.

Mason's head is bandaged. A tube draining blood and cerebral fluid is connected to a plastic bag with measurements marked in milliliters. Squeamishness drains away like our previous life.

Alan and I stand on either side of Mason's bed.

"Trish is sending an ambulance to come get you," Alan says in a voice that guards against danger with volume and stubborn cheerfulness.

I hold Mason's hand though he appears to be sleeping. His face is peaceful, relaxed. He doesn't seem to be in pain. The breathing tube in his mouth is like an inverted snorkel. His chest rises and falls at reassuring intervals.

He's alive. That's all I know.

# nineteen

# Jackson Pollock Faith

Austin texts that he and Sarah are parked outside the ER with my overnight bag. I make my way out to them and hug Austin through the car window.

"Mason's stable now. They've relieved the pressure in his brain." I don't want to scare my children. I don't want to scare myself.

"Do they know how long he'll be in the hospital?" Sarah asks. She looks a little older than her eleven years in the passenger seat with her teenage brother driving, but they both look out of place under the fluorescent streetlight at eleven p.m. on a school night.

"I'll let you know as soon as I do," I say.

"We'll be okay," Austin says. He knows that's my next thought.

"I love you. Grandpa should be at the house anytime now." I wipe away a tear that slips through my don't-scare-the-children face.

With the helicopter still grounded, Stanford's trauma team arrives in an ambulance with two pediatric ICU nurses and two EMTs. This is at once reassuring and troubling. Mason's situation is bad enough to rank the A-team and this level of emergency care.

There's no room for Alan and me in the ambulance, but Dr. Ruben reassures us that Mason is too heavily sedated to wake up during the ride. This will be a low-speed trip. Any jostling could upset Mason's compromised brain.

It's twelve a.m. The red taillights of the ambulance blur in the raindrops on the windshield, coming in and out of focus with the steady rhythm of the wiper blades. Fog hugs the bay, softening the city skyline just beyond it.

I turn on the radio as we come through the rainbow tunnel in Sausalito. A Bob Marley song begins as if by divine request.

"Don't worry about a thing. Every little thing's gonna be all right . . ."

Headlights illuminate the rain as it picks up in intensity.

"Do you hear this?" I turn up the volume.

Few cars pass in the northbound lanes of the bridge as we follow the silent ambulance south.

"Maybe we're being taken care of. Mason's doctors were having dinner together when you called. One call to activate Mason's whole team. Now this song." I'm gold-plating every positive sign into something I can hold on to, an anchor that might keep us from being swept right off the Golden Gate Bridge.

Bob Marley reassures me.

Alan doesn't respond. I'm disappointed by his lack of enthusiasm for spiritual guidance via KFOG radio.

Alan focuses on the ambulance ahead of us. We are steady, possessed of the kind of calm that comes from exhaustion and necessity, that is until we reach the other side of the toll plaza, and the ambulance turns left toward downtown San Francisco instead of right toward 19th Avenue.

"Where is he going?" Alan turns off the radio.

I dial the cell phone number that the EMT gave me. By now we're headed toward one of the steeper hills on Divisadero Street, the angle so abrupt that gravity tilts our heads into the headrests. I brace in sympathy for Mason.

"This isn't the easiest way to get to Stanford," I say when the EMT answers.

"This is the route the dispatcher mapped for us," he says.

"But the hills are steep this way."

"The neurosurgeon said Mason needs to be kept as still as possible," Alan yells across the car into my phone.

"He's secure in the back, no problem, his vitals are all stable."

We are at 45 degrees cresting the hill. The EMT is kind, skillful in extricating himself from my call, not deviating from his dispatcher's course. We keep the radio off now. Alan and I resume our laser focus on the ambulance taillights ahead of us, cursing the hills and the stoplights.

At Stanford the CT scan is reviewed by Dr. Edwards, confirming that the new tumor growth imploded, leaving jagged vessels bleeding into Mason's brain. The neurosurgeon will remove the ruptured tumor tissue, but there's no time for mapping critical brain functions. We must rely on the surgeon's practiced hands, and the prayers of friends and friends of friends, generous people we'll never meet.

After six intolerable hours of checking the red power light on the surgery-center pager and pacing the cafeteria, we meet Dr. Edwards in a consultation room. His surgical cap is pushed up off his forehead. He musters a tentative smile as Alan, Mom, and I squeeze onto a purple loveseat.

"It was a difficult surgery, but Mason is stable. His vital signs remained strong throughout. We were able to remove the ruptured part of the tumor, but it was not easy."

I notice the sag around his eyes. He looks ten years older than he did six hours ago.

"How Mason does the next few days will tell us a lot. He could start to make improvements, or he could take a turn for the worse."

"But there were no complications during the surgery?" Alan asks.

"No, but we don't know the extent of the damage to his brain stem," says Dr. Edwards. "Mason might never wake up. That could be worse than dying. You would have to make some difficult decisions about how much care to provide."

Alan looks like he's going to be sick, which is exactly how I feel.

"But you achieved what you set out to do surgically?" Mom leans forward, elbows on her knees.

"Yes, but it's hard to say what will happen next. This will be a rough Christmas for your family." He pushes himself up from his chair, pats my shoulder, and leaves the room.

His words take the air out of me. I hear, but I don't believe because none of this can be true. It can't be. The little girl that was me holds up her hand in the universal stop position. This is not happening.

Mason is in a medically induced coma, though I refuse to think of it as an actual "coma." His brain just needs inactivity so it can heal from the bleed and the surgery. If he were conscious, he wouldn't tolerate a breathing tube down his throat. So yes, it's coma-like, but I'm quite sure that if we dial back the drugs, Mason would sit up in bed and ask for the TV remote.

A man with thick-rimmed glasses and a Santa hat pauses in front of Mason's glass-walled PICU room before I can pull the shades down. He motions to the wagon of toys he pulls behind him.

"Sorry," I say, as I lean out the door. "You can't come in. He just had surgery." I make it sound like surgery was an hour ago, not last week.

"No problem," he says, and he reaches into his wagon and pulls out a stuffed green frog. He hands me the toy.

"Merry Christmas," he says with a smile that shows that he really means it.

"Thank you." I do appreciate his effort, but every "have yourself a Merry Little Christmas" reminds me of how far away we are from such a thing. Still, the frog is proving useful. I stretch Mason's fingers over its green polyester fur to release his right hand from the tight balled-up fist that is its new default position, fingernails digging into his palm.

The neurosurgeons do their rounds each morning and afternoon to monitor how Mason's brain is recovering. The problem is Mason barely wakes up—sometimes he doesn't wake up at all. And Dr. Edwards doesn't consider it a hopeful sign when Mason vaguely opens his dreamy eyes just shy of halfway. Ten minutes prior to rounds, the nurse arrives to turn down the sedation that keeps Mason completely unconscious so that he can—*please God*—come to.

"Dr. Edwards will be here soon," I tell Mason. "It would be a really good idea to show him what you can do."

Dr. Edwards enters with his entourage of medical students, residents, and neurosurgeons. He's six inches shorter than anyone in the room, and he commands the attention of everyone here.

"Hi, Mason," he says loudly. "Time to wake up."

Mason's eyelids drift apart. The particular shade of olive green is familiar, but my boy is absent behind them.

"Can you blink for me?"

His gaze remains unfocused.

I hold my breath and will Mason to blink as if there is some connection between my brain and his eyelids. Nothing happens.

"Can you lift your hand for us? . . . How about your leg?"

Mason's eyelids drift closed as if the force of gravity is too much to resist. It's getting harder to convince Dr. Edwards that Mason is with us.

"Is ten minutes long enough for him to wake up from the drugs?" I ask.

"It's plenty of time," Dr. Edwards says. His expression is sympathetic, but I don't want sympathy. I want reassurance.

The team retreats, most of them looking at their feet as they pass me. They gather outside our room where Dr. Edwards, no doubt, explains the characteristics of parental denial.

Mason's index finger glows E.T.-like from the red light of the pulse/oxygen meter taped there. The nurse turns the IV drip back on. Mason is with us, but he isn't.

Annie calls. I step out of the PICU to talk.

"He failed another neuro exam," I say, assuming she will agree with me that Dr. Edwards's grading scale is unnecessarily harsh. "The flicker of the eyelids doesn't seem to count for much. He wants to see 'intentional' brain activity."

"I don't think he's decided to come back or not," Annie says softly. "It's like he's in a hammock, biding his time between here and there."

I consider the image of my long-limbed son stretched out in a hammock. I envision palm trees and sunshine in this hypothetical place, outside the body that the nurses turn regularly to prevent bedsores. It isn't an altogether unpleasant image. A steady rhythm of waves replaces the incessant beeping of the monitors. I am absolutely sure that this is a vacation for Mason, a place to hang out while his body does the heavy repair work—a recess rather than a graduation.

"He'll come back when he's ready," I say.

Annie isn't the only one who doesn't understand that Mason isn't dying. When I was home over the weekend, an old friend pulled me aside in Walgreens and told me that I need to give Mason "permission to move on." But there are no decisions for us to make, no figurative or literal plugs to pull. Things are out of the realm of human choice, which makes most civilians very nervous.

I'm feeling more okay with this than not, which is unlike me. But faced with the choice between trusting that there is healing brewing inside of Mason's body beyond the understanding of even the most qualified, best educated doctors, or falling into the pit of hopelessness, I choose faith. It's not a polished Michelangelo faith. It's more of a Jackson Pollock kind of thing—an unformed, unshaped belief that there is Something at work here beyond our human intelligence.

"Dr. Fisher is 'cautiously optimistic,'" I say, wanting to make Annie understand. "He's had patients recover from worse, but he said it's a marathon, not a sprint."

"Okay, honey. Can you take a walk? Get some fresh air?"

Before hanging up, we pray for strength and healing. I promise to call her later. I need Annie too much to hold her lack of certainty against her.

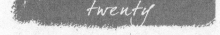

*twenty*

# Not Lost

When Mason was four, we attended a meditation retreat at a hotel in Palm Springs. I held Sarah on my hip while I went to the café for a snack of whole-grain cookies for the kids and chai tea for myself. Nearby, Alan worked on buying his way to serenity with a value pack of chanting CDs while Austin negotiated for a stuffed monkey.

That's when Mason vanished.

Alan searched the hotel lobby, the bathrooms. I checked the outdoor patio and the bottom of the pool. Mason was nowhere to be found. My mind defaulted to kidnappers disguised as middle-aged white women in saris.

I realized that I should have held on to Mason tighter.

We doubled back to the family area, where a guy with dreadlocks was playing the sitar. Mason sat in the corner, stacking cardboard blocks into a teetering wall.

"We thought you were lost." Alan's fear distilled into anger, then unsteady relief. "Don't ever wander off like that again!"

"But I wasn't lost," Mason said, balancing another cardboard brick on top of the stack. "I knew where I was all along."

---

"Mason, you're starting to freak people out. It's time to come back." I raise my voice, keeping the tone loving but firm.

I pull Mason's iPod out of my purse and tuck the buds into his ears. I pick a song he'd recently downloaded, "Airplanes" by B.o.B., and turn it up loud. "Like a shooting star. I could really use a wish right now . . ." I can hear the shadow of the music escaping his ear buds. At this moment I'm not worried about Mason losing his hearing.

My wish is that Mason come back right now. It's the only right answer. I'm standing on the edge of what I don't think I can survive, and I'm desperately trying to think nice thoughts to make *it*—destiny, fate, tomorrow's neuro exam—bend my way. I refuse to admit how unnerved and undone I am.

Veronica, our pastor from St. Andrew, braves Friday rush-hour traffic to visit. She looks at Mason in the bed with the soft eyes of a mother. It's seven p.m. and the nurses are changing shifts. We leave the room so we don't interfere. We walk the halls of the hospital. It's like being at school after hours—that feeling of being where you're not supposed to be. The offices are locked; the hallway is deserted.

"How are you holding up?" Veronica asks.

"I don't really know," I answer truthfully. I have no idea how I'm still able to stand and form sentences. It's unlike me to not have an answer, not to want to appear like I've got this—whatever this is. Usually I'd want Veronica to think I'm wise and spiritually evolved, one of her better congregants. Today, God seems like a faraway idea. I want to be filled with faith, floating in it, bathing in it. But I am just empty. Cold, dry, and empty.

"I do what I need to do. I miss Sarah and Austin, but I can't stand to be away from Mason. I pray all the time, but I'm still afraid." Then I whisper, "Mason isn't getting better."

I'm afraid to admit this too loudly.

"There's a story in the Bible about a man who brings his son to Jesus for healing. He says, 'I believe, but help my unbelief.' You can bring your unbelief to God. Invite God in right where you are."

That night I lay in the recliner next to Mason's bed repeating, "I believe, but help my unbelief."

My belief is a rope bridge over a canyon. There's wind and a thick darkness tugging at me from below, pulling me toward realities too terrifying to name. I can't look down, lest I lose my balance. But my muscles won't hold much longer. It hadn't occurred to me that God could fill the abyss just as God fills the sky.

On Christmas Eve the St. Andrew choir sings "Silent Night." I hold one arm around Austin and the other around Sarah. Alan reaches around the three of us. Messy, snotty tears flood my face. I don't try to stop them because I can't. We huddle together, around the spot where Mason is supposed to be.

My mom is at the hospital, most likely reading a book next to Mason's bed, and asking the night nurse if he washed his hands.

Annie stands behind me. I can feel her there.

Tonight we pass the peace with slim white candles. I touch my unlit wick to Alan's flame, then I share it with Austin and Sarah. The flame flickers upward, ebbing toward the church's vaulted ceiling.

Our house is lit with white Christmas lights. There is no hint of a missing family member or the held-breath anxiety that has moved into the rafters. Two nights ago, when Alan came home from Stanford at ten p.m., he and the kids untangled the strands of lights and laid them across the hedges lining the driveway, clipping them over the doorway.

Our neighbor Mary heard them and came out to help. For Alan, the Christmas lights mean that we are not giving in or giving up. If it were just me, I'd leave the holiday in the attic.

Growing up, I looked forward to Christmas, marking obsessively the Sears toy catalog as we did back then. I spent hours playing with the porcelain nativity scene, with the sort of enthusiasm other girls brought to their Barbie Dream Houses. I moved the shepherds, the three kings, and all the animals in procession, taking special care with the three-legged lamb. But the reality of it was more complicated, a seasonal recipe for disappointment, as times of high expectation often are. Mom would make the Polish *Wigilia* dinner on Christmas Eve, forming pierogi by hand after twelve-hour days at work, and crafting soup out of mushrooms my grandmother sent from the Polish store on Pulaski Avenue. That night we'd dress up. And Dad would begin the celebration with a festive cocktail—or four. Mom would pretend not to cry when he cursed and snapped at a small irritation. I would try to be wonderful enough to make both of them forget the argument so we could be as happy as Janie Swanson's family, who lived in a big white house under elm trees.

Maybe it's a reaction to a childhood of desperate exuberance and "acting as if" that makes me resist anything that feels forced or insincere. I'm good at stuffing my feelings, but I'm annoyed when other people tell me I should be happy on demand. Alan doesn't seem to have this problem. He has a streak of purposeful cheer that I alternatively admire and loathe. Alan says I get prickly around the holidays. I think he does. But it can be overwhelming, trying to give my children the antidote to my own childhood, to correct that cosmic karmic imbalance. I stay up late stuffing their stockings. Alan assembles the toys, and I write notes from Santa, complimenting the children on deeds well done in a blocky print that they won't recognize as mine.

Of course, I would never take Christmas away from Austin and Sarah, who are already sacrificing too much. We attempt to hold this year's version of the holiday three inches above the traumatic-childhood-event classification, hopefully avoiding adding another layer of hurt to what I can't seem to protect them from. I asked a friend if she and her family would help get a tree and decorate, and they made an occasion of it. Inside the house there's an eight-foot tree in its usual spot in the living room, decked out with red satin balls, tiny stuffed bears, green felt elves, and silver-framed photos of each child. Our five stockings hang from hooks on the mantle. There's some tinsel that I don't recognize lining the banisters of the staircases, cheerful gold glitz.

I hug Sarah. "It looks great," I say, mustering a cheerfulness that I keep in the bottom drawer of myself.

"Let's eat," Alan calls from the kitchen. He picked up Chinese food. Austin brings plates to the table as I grab napkins.

It's odd to see four plates, not five.

"How's Mace today?" Austin asks.

"Pretty good," I say. "He just needs downtime to heal, so they have him on a lot of drugs to keep his brain quiet."

"Yeah," Alan agrees. "Once they dial back the drugs, he'll be much more with it."

Sarah spoons lemon chicken onto her plate. "Who's staying with us for Christmas?" she asks.

"I am!" I say as happily as I can. "Dad's going back tonight. Tomorrow we'll go to Stanford and celebrate all together. Grammy is meeting us there."

I don't mention that Janice, aka Grammy, will be bringing the kids back home and that Alan and I will be staying at the hospital. She bought a one-way ticket from Pennsylvania last week. Tonight she's staying with Alan's brother and his family. Sarah nods, takes another bite of the fried chicken that glistens golden brown and honey glazed, like a dessert.

Alan and I catch each other's eye. We're a good tag team. It's how we've managed all these years with the kids and Alan's demanding job, all that travel. Both of us are capable people. It was hard to leave Mason tonight. I almost couldn't do it.

"I'll go back," Alan had said. "You should stay with the kids, be there Christmas morning."

It was a generous offer, a loving gift.

Mason won't, I refuse to say "can't," fully wake up. My world has shrunken to the size of his PICU room, really to the size of Mason's bed, his still body in that bed and the fragile tumor in his head. There's a dizzy feeling when I look away, like what happens when you bend over and stand up too quickly. The tumor has eclipsed me, just like my dad's alcoholism, just like my own. Food tastes like dust. Sleep is elusive. And while Mason might be biding his time between here and there, I'm trying not to disappear into a no-man's-land. Not that I wouldn't like to slip away into oblivion. That sounds nice. But my sober friends anchor me as do these children of mine, especially the boy in the bed who is depending on me not to give up on either one of us.

It's been a month now. Mason opens his eyes for seconds at a time, maybe a minute, in that newborn, underwater, slow way. We forget that this is an achievement because it's not enough. Dr. Edwards is still looking for evidence of intentional brain activity, and so far he remains unimpressed by Mason's water-baby act.

We trudge through one failed neuro exam, then another, hanging on to the threadbare prayer that today will be the day it turns around. I'm annoyed with Dr. Edwards because he insists we still don't know if Mason's coming back. It doesn't occur to me that he might be right. Alan is here when he's not at work. I'm hyper-focused: Mason will be back. I spend my days in a chair next to his bed, holding his hand, believing this until it's true.

"Blink if you can hear me, Mason," Dr. Edwards says, standing over him.

Mason's eyes open and shut and open again.

"He's blinking!" I yell.

Dr. Edwards nods with a detached expression. But clearly this is a point scored for Mason.

"Can you give me a thumbs-up, Mason?" Edwards asks.

Everyone in the room shifts their gaze to Mason's hand on the white sheet. It's as if we can see the energy gathering. There are two residents, three interns, and a nurse. Each of us is focused on Mason's thumb; each of us is silently rooting, *C'mon, you can do it.*

Slowly Mason's thumb extends away from his hand, then with a quick thrust pushes upward.

We all cheer. I jump and clap. I might be crying, too—I'm not sure. Alan pumps a fist in the air, high-fives one of the young interns. Dr. Edwards smiles. His face softens just the slightest. I notice it because I've been monitoring his every micro-expression for thirty-two days.

"It's progress," he says.

Dr. Edwards orders a tracheotomy and a gastric tube (G-tube), which confuses me because I still expect Mason to sit up and ask for a pint of Ben & Jerry's. Nobody has told me this is unrealistic. Then again, I didn't ask.

---

Now that the breathing tube has been moved to his throat, I can see Mason's unobstructed face. I notice that his front tooth was chipped, probably during intubation in the ER. He looks like himself but not exactly because there's no animation in his face, just a rubbery dullness to his cheeks and around his mouth.

Austin volunteers to spend the night with his brother since Alan just left on a late flight to New York. My sixteen-year-old son arrives with a laptop loaded with two seasons of *Friday Night Lights.*

I miss Austin, and I want to spend as much time as I can with him, but I'm nodding off in my chair.

"Go to the hotel, Mom. I can handle this," he says.

It's a generous gift to me—and to Mason. I decide to receive it.

We've rented a hotel room nearby where we shower and sleep when we can. I take a quick bath and pull on my pajamas. Every instant of sleep is limited, precious, and elusive. Just lying on the clean white linen makes me feel the tiniest bit hopeful. There is life outside of the PICU.

I wake up at four fifteen a.m. I heard someone knocking, maybe at the room next door. I check my phone. There are no texts from Austin. No missed calls.

Now I'm awake and alone in the dark, my mind pulling me along like a dog noosed by its own choke collar. It's five years from now, and Mason is still giving weak thumbs-up from a hospital bed. I jump forward forty-five years, and there's no one to care for him upon my tragic, imminent death. My mind skips to nursing homes with sex offenders as orderlies.

I try to remember if I bolted the door to my room. I rub the Mary charm. I long for my Sunday school faith, which wasn't faith at all; it was certainty. I remember the relief I felt when Sister Bernadette told us that God had a nice Son, a big-brother type, who would look after us. All I had to do was say His name, and He was there.

As a child, I was afraid of ghosts and shadows that seemed to dart out from empty corners. I awoke most mornings from horrible nightmares. The Sister's revelation that there was this magic God was good news for a scared child like me.

I chanted to myself, "Jesus, Jesus, Jesus," the way long-necked girls hold crosses in vampire movies.

These days I believe in a benevolent God, bigger than my human mind can conceive or define, but I still feel afraid. So I think of angels, muscular warriors with strong pelican wings. And I plead some more.

*Bring Mason back.*

Even when Mason's eyes are open, he's still far away. Now, with the trach and the G-tube, our lives have morphed into something I don't recognize. I'm so tired. I've tried so hard to be good, to believe properly and hence control my son's recovery. It's not working.

"Jesus," I say out loud, "I need to see something. Please let me know You've got this."

I try to sleep, but my head won't turn off. And when I open my eyes, a shape comes into focus on the ceiling, a gowned body, wings stretched overhead like two chubby arms and a perfectly round head. I blink hard in disbelief. I know the light must be shining up from a digital clock, reflecting through the lampshade. But the shape is indisputable—an angel. A paper doll angel. Under its vigilant gaze, I doze off for another hour.

I wonder if God comes to us in origami, random shapes, meaningless objects on a night table lit by a digital clock, if this is the point. But when I wake up in the morning, I notice that there isn't a digital clock on the night table. And as I remember it, my cell phone was facedown.

I can't explain where the light came from.

twenty-one

# The Next Right Thing

nnie and I sit at a table in a café across from the hospital. The place has seen better days. When I lived in Palo Alto after college, it was a high-end date destination. Now it smells like old carpet and spilled wine. I don't complain. I'm wildly relieved to be sprung from hospital duty and to see my dear friend across the table. I'm eating in a restaurant like a regular person, a luxury.

"I'll have the salmon special, please," Annie tells a dark-haired waiter named Steve.

"Same for me," I say as we both hand him our menus.

"We have a special chardonnay by the glass," he says.

"Not tonight," I answer, an inside joke for those of us who drank up our lifetime allotment at a young age.

"Lots of water, please," Annie says.

Steve retreats to the kitchen. Annie and I exhale together.

"Are you getting any sleep?"

"Not much. When my brain finally shuts off, my dreams are crazy vivid. Not all bad, but still. A few times I've dreamt that I'm in a VW bug on Highway 17, with an old friend. We have a six-pack of beer and a Duraflame log in the back seat. We're headed for Santa Cruz, and it feels like pure joy. Then I wake up."

I decide not to mention the angelic appearance via lightshow on my hotel ceiling the week before.

"It's about escape," Annie says. "Outrunning the pain."

This is probably true. I want a way out. The exhaustion and fear have become as much a part of me as my stick-straight, now gray-streaked hair.

"It's unrelenting. No end in sight. Completely out of my control."

"And there's this new Mason being born," she continues. "It's almost like starting over."

"Well, this labor is taking considerably longer then the first one, and there's no pain relief. Not for me, at least."

I think about Austin's birth, a long, intervention-ridden twenty-three hours. The second time around, I was determined to find ways to make the birth easier on me and the baby. This included seeing a hypnotherapist, who taught me that for every contraction, however intense, I'd always get a break to relax and recover.

"I thought I could endure just about anything after giving birth to three babies, but then I always knew the pain wouldn't last forever. With Mason I thought I'd be split in two, but in three hours there he was—nearly ten pounds of him."

During labor with Mason, I felt cheated when I didn't get the break in between contractions that the hypnotherapist promised. Then the midwife locked eyes with me and said, "You're not getting a break because your baby is coming really fast." I didn't complain after that.

That's how I met Mason.

Now it's thirteen years later and I've spent six weeks in the hospital trying to find him again. The pain is compounded by not knowing when it will end. But I'll labor as long as it takes.

I may not be good at letting go, but I'm skilled at stubborn, grippy, not giving up.

Steve delivers our dinner plates trimmed with tender broccoli stalks and lemon wedges. I cut into the pink fish, moist and perfectly grilled.

"Right now, just eat your salmon and drink a lot of water. Apple juice is good, too, just like in actual labor," Annie says. "Believe me, if I were God's West Coast representative, we'd have a totally different situation here. I promise you that."

"I know, right? Can we just make a list of all the people who should be off the grid in ICU limbo instead of Mason and these other kids? The world would be a much better place if certain grown-ups were absent for a couple months—or longer."

"It's just wrong," Annie affirms.

"Well, there's a reason I'm not God. I'd be all judgment and retribution, but at least the kids would be okay," I say, attempting a certain humility. Really, I believe I'd do a much better job than whatever divine force is supposed to be at work right now. First I'd fix the little girl with the burns next door to us in the PICU. Then I'd get rid of all the brain tumors and cancers—*poof*—gone. After that, I'd start mending bones and birth defects.

"It can be too hard for us mothers, even on a regular Sunday. And this is just beyond too much." Annie pauses for a sip of water. "Don't worry. I'm not going to say anything hostile, like 'God isn't going to give you more than you can handle.'"

This is just what I need—the acceptance of a good friend who doesn't try to put a shine on a dull ache. This nourishes me more than all the omega-3s in the fish. A good friend listens, then defies reason by finding an excuse to laugh, because that is the most not-alone you can be.

On a Tuesday afternoon the stars align, and we're finally moved out of the PICU. In Mason's new room is a bench that doubles as a parent's bed, under a big window overlooking treetops. I feel something like bliss when I lie down.

It's a rare moment of calm.

Mason dozes. His cheeks are flushed from the moist oxygen being pumped into his trach. There's a light overspray that gives him a twenty-four-hour-a-day facial. His skin, once prone to breakouts, is now flawless. This makes him look even more like an eerie, wax-museum replica of himself.

No longer constantly sedated, he wakes up on his own more and more. Today he opens his eyes as his nurse pours a can of liquid nutrition into his G-tube bag.

"Good morning, Mason!" she jokes, because the sun is setting outside.

Mason blinks.

He has yet to speak. It's my job to remind everyone that he had a breathing tube, then a tracheotomy. Of course he couldn't talk under those circumstances. But I am starting to understand something else is going on. Mason doesn't form words. He doesn't try to communicate that way. Mostly he blinks or slightly moves his head or his left hand. The other parts of him are not moving. Not yet.

"Would you like to watch TV with your dinner?" I ask.

He moves his head slightly, which I take as a yes. I flip through the channels and settle on *Seinfeld*.

"Okay?"

He blinks.

I pull a chair up next to his bed, open my laptop, and begin googling rankings of rehabilitation facilities. My current mission is to find a neurological rehab center where Mason can learn to walk, talk, and eat again. We sit side by side, each absorbed in our separate screens, almost like a regular mother and son.

Mason has been watching *Seinfeld* for about fifteen minutes when Dr. Edwards arrives for the evening exam.

"Hey, Mason," Dr. Edwards says. "Nice room. Can you give me a thumbs-up?"

I reach for the remote to turn down the TV volume. George is complaining loudly, and there is a rush of laughter from the television. Then a laugh comes from behind me.

It's Mason.

"Now that was intentional brain activity!" Edwards exclaims.

For the first time since Mason's hemorrhage, I see the neurosurgeon grin. I'm hugely relieved and also annoyed. I've known all along that Mason has been with us even if he's been deep underwater much of the time. Now that Dr. Edwards has seen it for himself, it is officially true.

It's difficult, some would say impossible, to manage what I can't control. Not just brain tumors but people. I can't care for Mason by myself, I'm more dependent on others than I've ever been. There are the people I know and love, my family and friends, who I fear wearing out. Our doctors, most of whom I love and whose safety I've begun to pray for. The nurses who become fast friends in twelve-hour shifts. And then there are those who won't give me their real names on the telephone—the ones who work at our health-insurance provider. These nameless individuals have disproportionate power over Mason's fate. Now I'm being introduced to the rehab people, those therapists and doctors who will bring Mason back into the suit of himself. And Mason has to strike just the right tone. He needs to be injured enough to need help but not too hurt to receive it. I have to strike the right tone, too; these people have to *want* to help us, all of them.

I've tried to outgrow people-pleasing, that tendency to gauge others' reactions and tell them what they want to hear despite any inconvenient, contrary feelings that might live inside of me. Now that my son's survival depends on the kindness of strangers, I've become a contortionist so that people will give us what we need. I am desperately nice, exhaustingly accommodating, and pleadingly wonderful, until I'm not.

Alan and I visit a San Francisco rehab just east of the Haight. Walls of windows overlook vistas of the city, the Golden Gate Bridge, and the Financial District. It's perfect, and we could sleep at home again. The admissions director is sympathetic to our situation, but they've never admitted a patient younger than sixteen, and Mason won't even turn fourteen until May.

When I arrive back at the hospital, I lean down and kiss Mason's forehead.

"We just saw an amazing rehab," I say. "They have therapists who specialize in brain injuries. Your friends could come see you."

There's a slight uptick on the left side of Mason's mouth, a micro expression, which I have started to recognize as a smile.

Megan, the hospital discharge planner, knocks. "I just saw an amazing rehab," I explain. "They're looking into whether they can take someone Mason's age."

"I'm afraid you don't have time for that," Megan says. "I just spoke to your insurance company. They've decided that Mason no longer needs hospitalization."

I've had endless fantasies of rolling Mason out the hospital doors, loading him into my car, and driving away fast. There are glitches in my plan. First, Mason can't sit up. Second, to go outside, he needs a special screen for his new trach so bugs don't fly into his lungs; I don't know where to buy these trach screens. The speech therapist has promised to bring us one tomorrow so we can take him outside on a patio in one of the hospital's reclining wheelchairs.

That night Mason's temperature spikes to 104. His nurse, Maggie, double-checks the thermometer. I brush the hair off Mason's sweaty forehead, noticing that his eyes are fluttering from left to right. Then his body stiffens. I ring the emergency button, and Maggie races off to grab the appropriate drug. Holding Mason's hand, I summon a calm I don't feel. I tell him, "We're riding a big wave together. It pulls us under, but it will always push us back up to the surface where the air and the birds are . . ."

Maggie injects anti-seizure medication into Mason's central line. The crisis passes, for now.

"Well, at least they're not going to kick us out of the hospital," I tell Alan, noticing that my thinking has taken on a new and undesirable twist.

Two days later Megan catches me before I can hide in the bathroom. I've been avoiding her calls.

"I know it's super busy around here," she says, "but I talked to your insurance company again. You need to stop visiting facilities and pick one."

The admissions director at the San Francisco rehab calls. Their insurance carrier refuses to make an exception to the age rule. He mentions a rehab facility in Houston that's known for their neurological program, and they work with children.

But how can we possibly move to Texas?

My sober friends talk about doing "the next right thing." I can't think of a way that moving Mason to Houston can possibly work, but I take each next step, waiting to hit a wall that will reroute us to the general rehab closest to my mom's house, which would be convenient, if far from ideal.

I'm sure Alan will agree that it's too far. Texas is two thousand miles away. We have two other children. Alan has a job.

"I can schedule a stopover on my way to that conference in Miami next week," my husband says. "I'll see if I can get a tour."

I call the health-insurance carrier so they can tell me that the Houston rehab isn't in our network. But it is.

I trade calls with air ambulance companies, getting a quick education on types of medical planes and crew certifications. It is amazing how easy it is to charter an airplane. The only problem is how to pay for it. Luckily, we still have some savings.

"It's our only good option right now," I tell Annie on a late-night call, clutching my optimism the way my grandma held her purse on the bus.

"But how is it going to work? What about Austin and Sarah?"

"I don't know exactly how we'll do it, but the pieces are coming together. And they specialize in brain injuries. They're saying we'll be amazed by the progress Mason's going to make once we get him there." I'm not answering Annie's question. I don't want to think about how much I'll hate being away from Sarah and Austin, from Annie and her questions, from my life. I have to focus on finding the people who know how to get Mason back.

Admitting I don't know how I'll manage is new to me, especially when it comes to my children. I always believed that I was in charge. Faith was something I thought I had—something I could tuck into my wallet along with my AAA card. What I need now is a faith that binds to my red blood cells, like an iron supplement.

As it turns out, "I don't know" is a profound spiritual answer.

There is a relief in this moment of overwhelm. Because once I dig out from underneath my good ideas and "what I think I know for sure," I find a knowing that is oddly comforting: perhaps there is Someone who has all power—and maybe it's not me.

# Take Off

Mason leaves the hospital on Valentine's Day, nearly two months after he was carried through these same doors by another ambulance crew. He squints into the sunlight as the EMTs push his gurney outside, then smiles his new left-sided half-grin. His eyes are open and focused though he still can't talk or sit up by himself. It's hard to know how much he understands.

"We'll be right behind you," Alan reassures as the EMTs close the door.

One more time Alan and I follow an ambulance in low-speed pursuit. But not because of Mason's fragility. This time we move without haste because we're downshifting into marathon pace, sure and steady.

My mother-in-law, Janice, who has been taking care of the children, the pets, and the house, has returned to Pennsylvania, and I hired a cheerful twenty-seven-year-old nanny named Ashleigh. My parents will take turns staying with Austin and Sarah on the weekends. Alan will come to Houston whenever he can.

Austin, Mom and Art, and Dad and Cecelia meet us on the

tarmac of the small airport where the air ambulance awaits. Leaning over Mason's gurney, they take turns kissing his cheeks and forehead, squeezing his hands. Mason's eyelids are flickering. He's getting tired.

Then it's time for Alan and me to get on the plane.

I hold on to Austin as long as I can.

"It's going to be great," Dad says, his voice cracking. I hand him the minivan keys. He and my brother, Tom, have volunteered to drive it to Houston for us.

"I love you," Mom says, wiping away tears with a wadded-up tissue. "Let me know when you want me to come."

"Thank you," I say. "I love you."

I hug Cecelia and Art. Each of them has shown up for inconvenient hospital shifts, never complaining about late-night calls and constant demands. This patchwork family of mine has proven to be everything we need. Swiping tears with the back of my hand, I wonder what it will be like to be too far away to call Mom or Dad to come over *now*.

I don't know a single person in Houston.

I knew the plane would be small, but I'm surprised by how small it is. The pilot introduces himself, and we buckle ourselves into a pair of seats behind Mason's gurney. EMTs Jim and Virginia set up Mason's monitors, then strap themselves into the jump seats on either side of him.

I kneel next to Mason and rub his free hand between mine.

"We're flying to an amazing rehab. They're so excited to get you moving again." I brush a hair off his forehead.

I think I see his face twitch in response. We're so lucky to have this chance, I remind myself. Then I pray that we won't all die in a fiery crash, pointing out to God that this would be a horrible ending to the story. Worst-case scenarios aren't as far-fetched as they once seemed.

Virginia starts Mason's *Seinfeld* DVD on a miniature TV and elevates his head just enough so he can fall back asleep when his next dose of painkillers takes effect. Jim passes us a small box of snacks—nuts and a Frito-Lay variety pack—a nod to the fact that this ride is costing us as much as a private jet, if we were the kind of people who did that sort of thing.

Alan buckles in next to me and smiles. If he's afraid, he's not showing it. He's also not showing the sting that I'm pretending not to feel after our recent disagreements.

Last week we managed a dinner out, just the two of us. We had a total of two hours to check romance, love, and marriage boxes. Instead, we had a fight. There's so much to disagree about that I can't remember what tipped us into an argument. It's like a multiple-choice test and the answer is always "D. All of the above."

"You're never on my side," he fumed. This wasn't entirely true. But I felt the heat rising off of him, like steam on a hot tub. I might've suggested that he call a therapist to talk through some of *his* issues.

I'm aware that my "judgmentalness" and compulsive need to be right are not among my most attractive qualities. Both stretched beyond capacity that night; we sat in silence when the waitress delivered our meals.

Alan is a big man in a big world. He works with women who go entire days without crying. Unlike me, those women probably smile when he walks into a room. They wear nicely cut suits and clever heels. I can see them laughing at his jokes and pretending not to notice the peppercorn between his front teeth.

We chewed in silence. Then Alan reached across the table, and I put my hand in his.

"It's really hard," he said. I nodded. I did get it, like no one else probably could.

I offered him my last shrimp. He passed me some French fries.

I wonder, is it even possible to be happily married when neither one of you is happy?

As the plane's engine revs up for takeoff, I watch Mason's monitor, noting his heart rate and blood pressure. I want those monitors to give me more information, including whether my two children at home are lonely or afraid and if the tie that binds Alan and me can endure what lies in front of us.

Alan squeezes my hand, then sets his computer up on his lap. I close my eyes and grip the armrests as our little metal capsule hurtles into the sky.

We land at a small private airport in Houston while the sun is shining through a haze of smog, giving the horizon a hot, yellow glow. It's a good thing we're here, I remind myself. Once we disembark, I climb into the waiting ambulance next to Mason while Alan picks up a rental car.

The hospital is institutional but not drab. There's a whiteboard on the door of each room with the patient's first name written in dry-erase marker. I can't help but glance into the rooms as we pass. There's the chatter of TVs. People sitting in beds, wheelchairs, and recliners (most older than I am); balloons and flower arrangements adorn bedside tables.

The EMTs push Mason's gurney through the hallway. A tall nurse in a maroon uniform greets us. "Welcome! My name is Martha."

"This is Mason Reid. We just arrived," I say.

"We have Mason in room 309." She leads us down the hall. One side of the room is clearly lived-in, with a stack of T-shirts folded on the bed, a bag of potato chips, and a liter of Coke on the bedside table.

"Mason will be sharing a room with Eli," Martha explains. "Eli is 15."

The EMTs transfer Mason to his new bed. Eli's family have claimed the bed next to the window and bathroom, as the first person in a room is apt to do.

"You have a roommate," I tell Mason. "A boy just like you."

The notion that there could be someone like Mason is still new. For once, he won't be alone in his situation. A nurse checks Mason's vital signs, records the medications he is on, and schedules him for a baseline CT scan.

———

"Hi." Eli waves from his wheelchair. He's thin and pale, wearing the kind of helmet that's worn after a craniotomy. His smile is even, and his speech is clear.

Mason stares vaguely in Eli's direction. No smile, no nod, much less a hello. I jump in with the desperation of a helicopter mom on the first day of kindergarten.

"Nice to meet you. Mason and I just got off a plane from San Francisco."

The man behind the wheelchair says in a soft drawl, "I'm Eli's dad, Anthony. We've been here for six weeks now."

"Are you from around here?" I ask.

"We're about five hours away. My wife stays home during the week with our daughter."

"I used a walker today," Eli says, propelling himself into the room.

"That's amazing," I say, envious and a little hopeful.

Mason stares blankly at Eli, and I'm grateful for the smile Eli gives Mason before he and his dad retreat behind the beige curtain that divides the room in two.

A woman in a lab coat arrives, juggling a manila folder and a cell phone, her short black hair grazing her collar. She speaks quickly.

"I'm Dr. Hill. Welcome." She lays a reassuring hand on Mason's forearm. "You must be tired after that trip."

Dr. Hill (not her actual name) is the physiatrist, a medical doctor trained in rehabilitation. She and I have spoken over the phone. Mason gives her the same vague stare. She smiles and turns to me.

"We jump right in around here. Our goal is to wean him off of any medication that makes him groggy." She continues, "We need you awake, Mason. You'll be out of bed every day and dressed. No lying around here!"

Dr. Hill reminds me of the mothers I sit with on the bleachers at Austin's basketball games: smart, self-assured, and pleasantly over-whelmed. This reassures me more than the hospital's impressive rating.

"I'll see you tomorrow afternoon," she says, her phone vibrating in hand. "Rounds are from three to five p.m."

Alan arrives a little while later and hands me a bottle of apple juice and a bag of cashews, our convenience-store dinner.

"Nice room, Mace. You've even got your own TV."

I muster the enthusiasm that I'd like to be feeling right now. "You just missed Dr. Hill. Therapy starts first thing tomorrow."

"Sounds good. You can stay in the hotel tonight," Alan says, offer-ing me an alternative to the sleeping recliner situated between Mason's bed and the closet door.

"Are you sure?" I ask.

The thought of staying in this room, with Eli and his dad, and uncertain access to the bathroom makes me want to cry, and the tears remind me of Sarah and Austin at home, which makes me want to sob. It's a lost, untethered feeling that reminds me of being sent away to summer camp at age ten.

"I'm sure," Alan says.

I often don't give Alan credit for volunteering for some of the toughest hospital shifts. Tonight I feel appreciation in the core of me.

"Thank you. I'll be back by five so you can get some rest before Mason's therapy." I kiss Mason on the cheek and give Alan a linger-ing hug.

Marriage doesn't always fit a shape sorter: happy, sad, in between. Maybe these moments of generosity are the payoff, giving and receiv-ing, especially when we're tired, afraid, and it's inconvenient.

*twenty-three*

# Until Tomorrow

My first night in Houston comes with a warning: a notecard taped inside the door reads, "Use deadbolt. Do *not* sleep with window open."

That's after a drive across a strange city, to what turns out to be a semi-sketchy hotel. I enter my room and lock the door behind me. I put my suitcase in the bedroom. I step into the shower, taking care not to let the plastic curtain touch my skin. The towels are stiff, but at least they smell like bleach.

As I dry myself off, I realize that I'm shaking. I'm so far from anything that anchors me. I want to scream or cry or run away. I'm supposed to believe in the wisdom that got us here, the doctors who accepted Mason into the program, and, of course, God. But right now all I feel is alone in this scary hotel room, where even sitting on the bedspread requires a faith I don't have.

I've always feared breaking down. This is one more thing that spurs me to be ultracapable. My great-grandmother Bernice started screaming and crying one day and couldn't stop. I visited her in the

Illinois State Hospital back when I was seven. I handed her a package of handkerchiefs embroidered with tiny purple violets, an unintentionally ironic gift that my mom bought at Woolworth. I smiled at the round-faced woman, who looked at me with kindness but no recognition. The room smelled like industrial-strength disinfectant, a scent that reminds you you'd leave this place if you could.

Early on I learned not to surrender to feelings like sadness, rage, or terror; to maintain a strong and pleasant exterior, a Teflon shield that would keep anyone from abandoning me in the locked ward. When I was a child, this felt like a real risk. The responsibility on my thin shoulders was enough to topple a less-capable girl. I had to keep it together so Mom wouldn't be so sad and Dad wouldn't leave. Adding to the heaviness was the secret that I couldn't tell anyone, not even God. So I built a fortress. I would be extra smart, doubly capable. I would cap off inconvenient feelings like an oil well, relegating the unpleasantness to unseen, subterranean places.

Right now my fortress is cracking. I can't keep it together. I toss the sticky comforter off the bed and climb under a caramel-colored velour blanket, clutching the bulky TV remote like a pacifier. The television gets three stations: local news on two of them and a CSI show on the third. I toss the remote aside and grab my phone.

Annie answers on the first ring.

"I hate it here. I don't know how I can stay." I start to cry, and I can't stop.

I tell her about the shared rehab room, the creepy guys hanging out across the street from the hotel. I don't mention that Mason didn't even acknowledge Eli when he wheeled himself into the room and yelled out hello. How Mason hid behind his frozen face, hearing but not hearing. I can't betray this, speak it out loud.

"It's a big mistake," I moan. "We shouldn't have come here."

"Right now it's just about getting through until morning," Annie says. "Burning through the hours. With any luck, you'll pass out from exhaustion. When you wake up, you'll see what you need to do."

I wipe my wet cheeks with a thin washcloth. "I can't be away from Austin and Sarah for a month. This is crazy. Awful. I need to come home. But it's not like I can put Mason back on a plane. He can't even sit in a chair for ten minutes."

"Let's see how it goes tomorrow. Right now let's just get to midnight. Do you want to pray?"

I sniffle, not sure that I want anything to do with the God who has delivered me to this hotel room, this life. But Annie doesn't wait for my approval.

"God, please be with Janine tonight. We know You are. Comfort her. Let her make it through till morning. Please protect her and Mason, Alan, Austin, Sarah, and the kitties." Annie pauses. "I'll leave my phone on my pillow. Call me if you need to. I'm right here."

"Thanks," I whisper.

I don't remember falling asleep.

---

My alarm wakes me before the sun at four thirty a.m. I dress quickly and thread my way back to the rehab through dark, unfamiliar streets.

As I approach Mason's room, I hear Alan snoring. I don't want to wake him, so I find a seat in the lounge area next to the nurse's station where there's a coffeepot and a television. The blackness outside the window morphs into lighter shades of blue. An early-morning traffic report scrolls across the TV screen, throbbing veins of unfamiliar highways clogging as the sun rises over this vast city.

"You doing all right, honey?" A tiny African American woman rests a hand on my shoulder. "I'm Mavis. I've been an aide at this hospital for thirty-five years now."

Her bouffant reminds me of my grandmother. Estelle, my dad's mother, was just under five feet tall and thin, which was the greatest compliment you could give her. She always smiled when she saw me, so sure I was someone special. She rubbed my back and offered me pink Nestle Quik. Estelle never broke down like her mother-in-law, Bernice. Instead, she retreated inside herself, sucking deeply on her Marlboros, washing every cell in nicotine.

Miss Mavis is about the same height and pretty too. She doesn't smell of cigarettes or Norell perfume, but she's thin and of grand-motherly age.

"I'm okay," I say, although my eyes are gritty and swollen.

I tell Miss Mavis that we've come all the way from California, that Mason's brain tumor hemorrhaged, that he is here to learn to walk, talk, and eat again. Her sympathetic *uh-huh* registers just the right note. No pity here. She's matter of fact: there's work to be done, and we're in the right place to do it.

"You need anything, just let me know," Miss Mavis says.

I want to go home with her, sleep on her couch, and eat her soup. "Thank you," I say.

"He will give you the strength you need," she responds with confidence that inspires me since it comes from seeing many people recover from so many states of brokenness in all her years on the job.

I believe her. There's strength in her face, a patina acquired over years of giving and not giving up. It brings me back to my grandma, who worked as the coat-check lady in the beauty parlor at Marshall Fields on State Street. Estelle loved style and glitz, pretty things that shined brighter than any shadow that nipped at her well-appointed ankles. She and her four sisters wore hats with matching handbags, coordinated heels and stockings. For forty years she rode the bus to work with her hair done and her nails buffed. Back then Chicago's matrons checked their furs and packages with Estelle while getting their weekly set and style. At Christmas Mom would take my brother and me downtown, and we'd eat lunch under the Great Tree in the

Walnut Room. It's what made me love cities—the bustle, the mosaic ceiling, the perfumed ladies, green paper shopping bags, and Frango Mints. I loved it all. It was 1970, my mother's hair was champagne blonde and her eyeliner a precise swoop of liquid brown that matched her eyes. It was important to be the daughter of a pretty mom. It meant there was hope, especially when my front teeth came in large and protruding.

"You're beautiful," Grandma insisted at my First Communion. She was so sure, it broke something inside of me. I looked down at the perfect white lace dress my mother sewed with a matching veil, crying at the hopelessness of it all. After that, checks for $50 or $100 arrived every month with "Janine's teeth" written in Estelle's filigree script on the note line.

My grandmother gave me something precious. I wouldn't know how rare until years later. It wasn't just the teeth money or those fresh new twenties she tucked into greeting cards. It was what she conveyed when she looked at me that landed deep inside, deeper than all the hurt and strangeness of my childhood. It was joy and worthiness I saw in her eyes. Radical acceptance. If there had been words, they might have been, "I know it's really hard, but you're wonderful, more wonderful than you know." All she had to do was look at me.

Estelle even managed that expression after taking care of my brother and me when our parents were on vacation many years later. That Wednesday night, fifteen-year-old me climbed out my second-story bedroom window to meet a boy. Any fear of falling and impaling myself on the car antenna in the driveway below was dimmed by a hormone-impaired teenage brain that favored acceleration over brakes. When I returned home later, the window in my bedroom was closed and locked, as were all the doors to the house. I could see Grandma through the kitchen window, wearing her pink robe. She gazed out into the darkness where I hid and waited—for a very long time. Eventually I managed to wake my brother, who let me in his window.

The next morning Estelle stood at the kitchen sink, running the tap hot for her Sanka. She never said a word. There was no "I'm so disappointed in you," or "What kind of girl climbs out her bedroom window on a school night?" I got it. I wasn't getting away with anything, not on her watch. And most remarkably, she still looked at me the same way.

I hope it's in the DNA, something I can pass on. That I'll work hard to get my people whatever they need, and that my gaze will always reflect that they are worthy and enough.

She liked Alan, a lot. At our wedding she made him promise to take care of me. He said he'd do his very best. That last Christmas she spent with us, she had a hearing aid device that looked like an old-fashioned Sony Walkman with a headset and a microphone. Once three-year-old Mason found that mic, he wouldn't let it go. He sang loudly and danced, like Tom Jones in a droopy diaper. Grandma laughed even as she cringed from the volume.

I'm not sure my dad saw that same unconditional reflection in her eyes. She wasn't perfect. Then again, neither am I.

---

Half an hour later Alan emerges from Mason's room, bloodshot and pale. Turns out Eli and his dad share passions for watching the all-night wrestling channel while talking on their cell phones. I pass my husband the hotel key, and he hobbles down the hallway like an extra in a zombie movie.

By nine a.m. a nurse's aide named Robert has Mason washed, dressed in sweatpants and a T-shirt, and his teeth brushed. His morning meal hangs from a metal pole. Mason's face remains impassive, a mask of itself, but his eyes are open.

His occupational therapist, Laura, pushes a wheelchair into the room, then leans over to make eye contact with Mason. "I hear you came all the way from California."

Mason's blank stare doesn't affect her either. Laura is in her late twenties with smart, practiced hands.

"Today we're going to get you set up in your own wheelchair," she says. It's one of those paraplegic chairs that supports every body part from head to feet. Eli's chair looks like an Indy race car parked next to it.

"We'll start with a chair like this and adapt it as you need less and less support," she explains.

"Wow," Alan says. "You'll be racing Eli down the hall before you know it."

For the next week Alan and I swap night shifts and therapy shifts. So far Mason has thrown a ball and said his first word, and I hear it with the same giddy thrill that I did the first time he formed this same word some twelve years ago.

"Mason, can you make the shape of the word *mom* with your mouth?" his speech therapist had asked, her precise diction softened by a hint of Texas accent.

Mason slowly turns his head toward me.

"Mom." He spits out the word in one forceful exhale, his face pulling into that one-sided half-grin.

"Mason! That's amazing!" I shout.

It feels like someone just turned on the lights inside me. A shard of happiness slices through the persistent gloom I pretend not to feel.

The words are in there. And he's beginning to find them.

Alan books a flight home with a plan to return to Texas in two weeks. I tell myself I can do this, but I'm afraid and already a little lonely.

Fortunately dad and my brother, Tom, arrive that Saturday. They've driven our minivan across four states to deliver it to us.

"You made it!" I say, hugging them both. "Mace, look who's here!"

"Hi," Mason says, slowly but intelligibly.

"Hey, Mace!" My dad hasn't heard Mason's voice in months. "How you doing, buddy?"

Mason grins.

"Mason, you look great." Tom pats his shoulder. I follow my brother's eyes, seeing the trach hole in Mason's neck as if for the first time, the gauze, and the plastic collar. Tom doesn't blink or look away. He has three kids of his own, the same ages as mine. He is a practiced and solid dad.

The last time we were together, Tom's three children and mine posed for photos on the cliffs above the beach in San Diego. Mason was the tallest.

The three of us go out for Chinese food. Over fortune cookies, my dad offers to stay with Mason overnight. Another generous gift.

Growing up, I'd find apologies written in my dad's loopy handwriting on yellow legal pads that he left on the kitchen table. He detailed his regret about what had happened the night before, a lengthy double-sided explanation about why he'd yelled, punched the wall, thrown a plate, the reason, the excuse, and never once did he have it right.

When Dad sobered up, there remained a divide even after another handwritten note on yellow paper arrived in the mail. This time he said there was no excuse and he wanted to make it up to me as best he could. Gradually I started picking up the phone when he called, and he began cheering me on from whatever distance I needed.

Twenty-four years later he's someone I can count on when things get hard—when I need, well, my dad.

We slip into a comfortable routine though I know he needs more sleep. He is sixty-eight, but he's always been a young dad, and he refuses to let a number affect his attitude. Ten miles on his bike is a short ride.

"Are you sure you can do another night?" I ask.

"I'm fine," he says. "I'll sleep when I get home."

He leaves the next day, with a promise to return anytime we need him.

———

In Houston there are no familiar streets or people to remind me of who I am and where I belong. In some ways life is very simple. Every morning I walk from the rehab to our new "safe" hotel to shower and change. Then I weave through the maze of Medical Center buildings. On the way back I enter the chapel at the Methodist Hospital to pray. It's quiet, with an empty pulpit and stained glass lit by the windows of the hospital's sun-soaked lobby.

I cross myself, Father, Son, Holy Spirit, like I learned to do when I was three. My mind still defaults to "what ifs" and they're never cheerful pictures. I am not lifted out of this experience, yet every morning I pray; then I move my feet where they need to go.

"You'll be amazed," Norma, the nursing supervisor, tells me daily. I try hard to believe her.

Just yesterday, the respiratory therapist took the first steps toward getting rid of the trach. Mason's eyes are brighter, though his facial movements are uncoordinated, as if his eyes don't know that his mouth is smiling.

———

Alan arrives with Austin and Sarah, who are off school for the week. It helps to see Mason from their perspective. He *has* made progress.

"Mommy!" Sarah runs into my arms, and I pick her up even

though she's too big for this. I run my hands through her hair and kiss the top of her head.

"Hey, Mason," Sarah says. I can tell she's relieved to see him awake and wearing real clothes. Her voice shakes, but she seems strong and sure of herself.

"Hi," Mason replies weakly but with a smile.

"Mace, you look great," Austin says, looking taller than he did three weeks ago. It's the longest I've ever been away from either one of them.

"I hear you're on fire here. Good job," Alan says, leaning over the bed.

"Hi," Mason repeats, responding with the right word, quick and appropriate, though there's no inflection in his voice.

Later that afternoon, Molly, the music therapist, comes to Mason's room for his speech therapy session. The music is a way to trick Mason's brain into responding verbally, since this knowledge is stored on a different brain pathway than day-to-day speech. We each grab an instrument from her basket of tambourines, drums, and maracas.

"Mason, what are we going to sing today?" Molly asks.

"I bet you know this one." Molly strums familiar chords on her guitar and begins to sing. "He's got the whole world in His hands . . . ," and everyone except for Mason sings along. He stares at the drum in Austin's hand.

"Okay now, Mason's turn," Molly sings. "He's got the little bitty babies in His—" then hesitates, waiting for Mason to fill in the blank.

We hum and sway, shake, and shimmy, careful not to chime in ourselves.

"He's got the whole world in His . . . ," Molly repeats.

"Hands," Mason says, his voice soft and breathy.

I cry and laugh in one big burst. Alan and the kids cheer. Each word Mason pulls out of the void is a major victory. I wipe a tear away. *It's working*, I tell myself. *Being here is worth it.*

We manage to have fun, searching out the best tacos and barbeque in town, also beginning Mason's collection of University of Texas and Texas A&M T-shirts (not wanting to offend his Longhorn physical therapist or his Aggie occupational therapist).

Saying goodbye to Alan and the kids, I'm like a lost girl. Loneliness is a tide that ebbs and flows. It dissipates during the day, when I'm focused and busy. It's worse at night as Mason sleeps and I squirm in the sleeping chair, earbuds buffering out conversations in the hallway. I point my mind at Netflix, lest it travels into unwelcome, unproductive places.

I pray. I try to believe that I'm not as alone as I feel.

# Under Water

In the rehab gym I lift my six-foot-tall son out of his wheelchair and deposit him in a bed that's set up in the corner to resemble an apartment. I place my hands just so under his arms, squat, and pivot, moving all one hundred and eighty pounds of him. In this moment I feel like the superhero of my own story. It's a deliciously powerful feeling. I'm ready to flex my previously nonexistent biceps and do a little dance.

"Make sure you protect your back. Engage your core," Hannah, the physical therapist, coaches. "But good work."

"One more time, Mason?" I laugh. But Mason has dozed off in the bed, chin to chest. He's sound asleep. This morning he fell asleep in occupational therapy after throwing a ball three times.

*He had a big weekend with the whole family here*, I tell myself. *Who wouldn't be tired?*

"Do you have a headache?" I ask when he's settled back in his room.

Yes, he nods.

I tell Dr. Hill when she comes by on her afternoon rounds.

"He's always been prone to headaches, right?" she asks.

"Yes, but there's usually a reason," I say.

"We'll get you something to take that pain away," Dr. Hill says, as her phone vibrates in her pocket, and she excuses herself.

Mason's eyelids flicker closed. He came out of his hiding place just long enough for me to get a glimpse of him. I fear he's disappearing again, though everyone insists he's making progress.

<hr>

On Friday Mason is asleep when Alan arrives.

"Are you hungry?" he whispers.

"Sure." I realize that I ate a Larabar for breakfast six hours ago.

We cross the street to a nice restaurant with tablecloths and a menu that isn't posted on the wall. I tuck my black T-shirt into my jeans. Alan is wearing the suit he's been traveling in since dawn, Eastern time.

"So, Jel." Alan pauses, holding my hand under the table. The nickname is short for Jelly Bean, which Alan started calling me in the early days of our dating life for reasons neither one of us can remember. "When are you going to get a break?"

"Someday." I sip my iced tea.

"At least I can get away," Alan says. "You're always on."

I enjoy being acknowledged, appreciated even. I can't imagine not being with Mason every second, but how can I keep up the 24-7 vigil? This last thought is a whisper I pretend not to hear because my limitations as a human in a body might not apply if I pretend not to see them.

The waiter serves me a tall glass lined with four super-sized shrimp rising from a pool of cocktail sauce. I bite into the best shrimp I've ever tasted, which buoys my mood.

"The neuropsychiatrist said Mason was the most improved patient last week," I say. "He said Mason could make a full recovery."

"That's amazing," Alan says. "I know it's hard being away from home, but it's worth it."

"He's had a couple of rough days since then," I mention so Alan isn't surprised. But I don't dwell on it because I don't want Mason's setbacks to mean anything. We're tenuously poised, novices on a balance beam. I don't want to push Alan—or myself—over to the other side.

The next day we return early from speech therapy because Mason started to blink uncontrollably. Dr. Hill's diagnosis is "storming," a condition that's common with severe brain injury. New drugs are added to Mason's mix. He starts to throw up regularly.

"Oh, Mason, there you go again," Dr. Hill scolds. I know she means to be tender and funny, but her words land hard and cold.

Mason moves his head slowly in the doctor's direction, like a manatee in an aquarium. His eyes are open but only halfway.

"Mason seems really spaced out," Alan says.

"He just had a scan yesterday." I interpret Alan's concern as a criticism, as if I've let Mason become spacey on my watch.

Alan insists on a consultation with Dr. Hill.

"The ventricles look the same to me," she reassures, having reviewed the latest CT. We're worried about hydrocephalous, especially now because the blood from the hemorrhage could clog his shunt.

"I'm supposed to go home this weekend. Do you think that's a good idea?" I ask.

"Go home. Get some rest. Have a good time with your other kids. Mason is doing great." Dr. Hill puts her arm around me, and I chide myself for having doubted her. *We're just overly worried*, I tell myself, and who wouldn't be?

After four hours of delays and a cancelled flight, I board a plane that eventually lands in San Francisco. As I drive across the Golden Gate

Bridge, it's one of those picture-postcard days: the sky is a bright shade of California blue, and the bay is dotted with white sails skimming across the water. The mountains that line the coast are soft-bodied and lush green. Even though I left half my heart in Houston, I feel uplifted and relieved.

I love where I live.

Walking into my house is like slipping into my skin again. The dogs wag their tails madly. Sarah jumps into my arms. Austin piles on too. Ashleigh has eliminated the clutter on the kitchen counters. The mail is neatly stacked in a basket. I make a pot of macaroni and cheese on my own stove and go to a familiar grocery store and walk straight to the tampon aisle. I'm not lost, wandering, looking for things, apologizing for not knowing.

This might be heaven, when the ordinary grace of each moment is revealed in extraordinary focus. The clarity comes from the center of my being: the children, the daffodils pushing through the mud, the familiar sounds that become part of the quiet, people walking their dogs outside the window, voices from the TV downstairs.

For minutes at a time I forget that Mason isn't on the couch in front of the TV. I lie in my own bed with my own daughter curled up next to me. This bliss lasts exactly one hour. Then the phone rings.

"Mason threw up his dinner." Alan sounds angry as if someone, somewhere is to blame.

"Page Dr. Hill," I tell him, not knowing what else to say. Mason throws up regularly now, but he still tips toward improvement most days.

"He fell asleep five minutes into speech therapy." He sighs.

Mason's empty bedroom begins to throb like something out of a horror movie. I try to ignore it.

Sarah and I paint our nails and bake cookies. Austin stays home and watches movies with us instead of going out with friends. I maintain my fragile sense of well-being by forcing myself to stay where the pink toenails are. Time stretches and pulls like taffy. I catch myself staring at Austin instead of the TV. I can see a shadow of him as a grown-up—the man he will become. My children grow and change every day. I'm missing something when I'm not here, and I'm missing something when I'm not there.

On Sunday afternoon I wrench myself away. I stare out the plane's window, feeling my stomach grip into rehab gear.

Alan picks me up at the airport. His curly hair is sticking straight up, which means he's been pulling on it, a childhood habit that reappears when he's worried.

"Hill keeps blowing me off," he greets me. "But I know something isn't right."

I find Mason asleep in bed. Hannah brought him back early because he was so tired in physical therapy. I kiss his forehead. He looks at me with unfocused, infant eyes. I know it in my bones now. Mason has gone backward. He's here, and he's not.

Dr. Hill arrives. "How was your trip? Your husband has been very worried," she says in her one-wife-to-another way.

I don't bother with pleasantries. "How is Mason?"

"Great. Just look at him!" Her happy voice doesn't seem to apply to the boy who is staring at the wall next to his bed.

"He's not okay," I say. "This is not what he's like. We need to get him to a neurosurgeon, now."

"We're working on getting him an appointment," Dr. Hill says. "But you can relax. Despite what your husband might think, there's no emergency here."

What she doesn't know is that three feet away from her, on the other side of the bathroom door, Alan is e-mailing screenshots of Mason's CT scan to neurosurgeons here and back home.

"We need to get him to Texas Children's," I say, which is where our California doctors told us to go for a medical emergency.

"They don't have any beds," Dr. Hill says. "You can't just walk out of one hospital and into another. The insurance company won't allow it." Then she lowers her voice into an angry whisper. "You have post-traumatic stress, and right now your actions are hurting your child."

I look at Mason. His eyelids are fluttering oddly.

"Absolutely. I do have post-traumatic stress," I yell, "*and* we've got to get Mason to a neurosurgeon, *now*."

Dr. Hill leaves the room, swift and silent. Margaret, the nurse's aide, has been standing behind me observing the exchange.

"You are the mother. You need to do what you think is right," she says in a soft but certain voice.

Within twelve hours my unrelenting husband manages to land Mason in the emergency room at Texas Children's Hospital (TCH). Within a half hour of our arrival, neurosurgeon Dr. Curry diagnoses Mason with hydrocephalous. Mason is drowning in his own head, which explains his underwater appearance. Dr. Curry admits Mason and schedules him for surgery to replace the shunt in his brain. When updated, Hill explains that she was trying to get Mason transferred all along. I don't have the bandwidth to pursue the argument. I have PTSD after all, plus a child headed into emergency surgery.

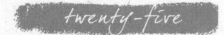

# twenty-five

# Evidence

Texas Children's Hospital is a well-funded, fourteen-story structure in the heart of the Texas Medical Center, lined with walls of windows, abundantly stocked playrooms, and a well-equipped patient gym. After Mason's emergency surgery, we move to a large corner room overlooking Fannin Street. The tall office buildings of downtown Houston sketch a jagged horizon; we are high enough that we don't hear the sirens below. The sunlight cheers me.

Mason wakes up. He looks at Alan and me, startled.

"You're at Texas Children's Hospital. They've just fixed your shunt. Do you feel better?" I ask.

Mason nods slowly. His eyes are clearer, with the slightest hint of curiosity, as he looks out the window. With the pressure relieved inside his brain, he sits up on the side of his bed for the first time in four months. When I move him to his wheelchair, he uses his legs to support himself instead of leaning his full weight on me.

"We'll get you back to rehab as soon as we can," Alan explains.

We're excited by the possibilities now. Though we had our difficulties with Dr. Hill, the therapists were great, and now we have

Dr. Curry nearby for medical support. It might not be the perfect scenario, but it's one we can work with.

While we're inpatient, the TCH Tumor Board reviews Mason's case, and the team recommends proton radiation. The oncologist explains that this type of radiation can be more targeted and less damaging to tumor-adjacent areas of the brain. We've looked into every possible treatment option from chemotherapy and radiation to pioneering studies in immunotherapy in Tel Aviv. Everything, except this. I am appreciative, but mostly I'm stunned and a little skeptical because how could there be something else? It's inconceivable that we'd add anything to Mason's lengthy rehabilitation, especially at this time. I also can't imagine inflicting more trauma on his brain. We thank the oncologist and tell him we'll consider the offer.

Alan and I read about proton radiation online. It turns out that there are only six proton centers in the United States. I feel something odd that I can't immediately identify—a fluttery, flashy optimism. Could this be the elusive God at work? It's a delicate hummingbird of a feeling, a whirl of color and movement, quick, beautiful, and easily missed. I've been not-so-patiently waiting for a miracle, or at least a change in the wind. Something dramatic and obvious would be nice. We wait. We pray. We gather information, believing that we'll know what to do next.

This time, communication from God comes in the mail. It's approval for proton therapy from our health insurance, no secondary review, no reflexive refusal. Thankful, we formulate a plan. Mason will get proton therapy after he finishes rehab. I envision us living in an apartment nearby, eating dinner together. Austin and Sarah can come for the summer. We prioritize. It's logical. The doctors agree.

To her credit, Dr. Hill welcomes us back to the rehab two weeks after we left. According to her, she got Mason to Texas Children's just in time, despite his parents' reactive and traumatized state. I choke down my irritation. I'll eat anything for Mason. It's like the TV show *Survivor*, only the stakes are higher. We're given the only available room, which happens to have a plastic garbage bag taped on the window of the door for privacy, along with an old sign warning of quarantine. I am determined not to let this get in the way of our beautiful plan.

"So, Mason, you gave us quite the scare," Dr. Hill scolds in a lighthearted way.

Mason's physical therapist has a new trick. She harnesses him into a man-sized walker that holds him upright so he can walk. Mason still has a face a Botox aficionado would covet—smooth, unanimated features that don't show the effort it takes him to lift one foot, then the next.

We all cheer as Mason moves across the gym. It's the best thing that has happened so far. I take pictures and text them to Alan. He's in New York. We've returned to efficient tag-team mode.

Back in his room, Mason naps. "Ow," he screams suddenly, grabbing his side.

I press the call button.

Dr. Hill presses the sore spot.

"Ow!" he yelps again.

"It's probably a pulled muscle from that workout. I'll get you some Tylenol."

The next morning, Mason looks pale. His forehead is warm. I call the nurse, who presses his side and elicits another yelp. The resident appears at Mason's bedside. She positions her hands over his sore spot, preparing to press on it again.

"Stop!" I bellow. "It's going to hurt. We don't have to make him hurt more than he already does. Something is really wrong. I'm putting him in that wheelchair and running him over to Texas Children's myself if you don't get him there right away!"

This is bigger than a pulled muscle.

"Okay," says the resident who had the bad luck of pulling this assignment. "I'll page the on-call doctor."

The steely clarity coming through me feels right and powerful. I unplug my phone and slip it in my purse. I eye the wheelchair parked at the door.

Within the hour an ambulance takes us back to TCH. Soon Mason is in a hospital bed with a drip of potent antibiotics to address the cyst that has developed in his abdomen where his shunt drains. Surgery is scheduled to remove the irritating hardware, the entire shunt apparatus that is now contaminated by infection. The surgeons will place external drains in Mason's brain, then replace them with new shunts in another surgery once the infection clears. I walk to the rehab to pick up our things—my electric teapot, Mason's clothes, the cards and drawings we'd taped to the walls. I know we won't be back.

My plan for Mason to finish rehab is a bust. He's sinking again under the haze of pain medication and more trauma to his tender brain. Back at TCH, Mason sleeps. The view from the new hospital room is all sky, white clouds and bright blue, but it doesn't cheer me. I take my phone into a deserted exam room, close the door, and call Joan.

"He's having two more brain surgeries," I tell her. The words catch in my throat.

"You don't think you can do it, do you?" Joan asks.

"I can't." It helps to know that someone gets it. We are in day one-hundred-something of Mason's hospitalization. Years into this cycle of clench, hope, and despair.

"But you *are* doing it," Joan says. "You are."

Joan is right. I am doing it. I *have* done it, through four hospitals, all of these brain surgeries, three close calls. But it's all too hard. Made worse by the ill-advised optimism I allowed myself to feel. That hummingbird of a feeling is now the captive of a sadistic cat.

I wipe my eyes on the hem of my T-shirt.

"I know you don't feel it, but God is there right now," she says. "It doesn't look like you think it should, but you're being cared for—and so is Mason—every minute."

I hope so. I mean, I think so. There's a gap in my faith. White space. My prayers echo in the unknowing place between what's happening and what I don't think I can survive. I wish God would appear like the Fabio Jesus statue in the Methodist Hospital lobby, or even the white-bearded, thunderbolt thrower who is represented in a remarkable spray-painted portrait on the hood of a Ford Taurus in the hospital garage.

Joan reminds me to pay attention to what's right in front of me. Evidence.

Dr. Curry met Mason in his exam room within a half hour of me threatening the resident at the rehab. A kind person at the United Airlines 1-800 number managed to get Alan rerouted to Houston on what was thought to be a full flight. And Joan answered the phone.

Cared for . . . maybe.

———

Surgery is scheduled, and the insurance approves Mason's next hospital stay. This is all I know right now. And despite the failure of all my previous plans, I want a new one, a detailed way forward that will guarantee that Mason comes back fully himself—and soon. A checklist would be nice.

I don't mind hard work; actually, I prefer it. I may have been the only girl in the fifth grade who kept a list of the Seven Sacraments in her pink vinyl diary. I made Xs next to those I'd completed—Baptism,

THE OPPOSITE OF CERTAINTY

Holy Communion, Confession—and Os next to those I was likely to complete, like Confirmation, Marriage, and Last Rites. The sacrament of Holy Orders was the only one I skipped because I was in love with Scottie Dean, and Catholic nuns married Jesus. They were very serious about this. But six out of seven was still in the A range.

This was the kind of big-picture plan I could get behind. I didn't want to end up in purgatory with the unbaptized babies. I liked babies well enough, but there had to be a reason my mom called it limbo. Maybe the fact that I spent my spare time considering ways to avoid eternal damnation—or limbo-like boredom—had something to do with my inferior social standing on the playground. I remember the day a friend turned on me, when she and one of the popular girls hid their whispers and giggles behind their hands as I approached. It was that nonspecific laughter that makes a girl run through the list of all the things that are wrong with her to figure out what might have been spotted. Was it the way my silver headgear clashed with the gold rims of my John Lennon glasses? Were my pants too short? Did I smell?

Now I know why the Greeks believed that the gods were petty and vindictive. I can see Athena whispering behind her hand to some lesser goddess, snickering, "Nice plan, Janine. Finish rehab. Get an apartment. Take Mason to proton therapy. Great idea." It wasn't a plan at all. I'd ridden a giant zigzag from hope to despair. This was no checklist. It was a dot-to-dot picture of an uncaring universe, a mean-spirited Rorschach test. The evidence? It goes both ways.

That fifth-grade part of me is preserved in a wallet-sized headshot. My teeth didn't protrude over my lips anymore, so I was able to take off my headgear for picture day and pass as the pretty girl that my grandma insisted I was. Also, Scott Dean asked me to be his partner for square dancing during PE class. With his long blond hair grazing the shoulders of his OP T-shirt, he smiled when we linked elbows and swung around. It was a moment of heaven, and it lasted just fourth period. But still. A few days later I was back in my bedroom after an orthodontist appointment. This time flipping through my Girl Scout manual working on merit badges, each with its own glorious black-and-white, words-on-paper checklist. I still have the green sash with embroidered badges neatly sewn up both sides, testament to my competence in task completion but inconclusive regarding my ability to shake the axis of the planet.

***

Mason is wheeled away, then deposited back into his hospital room after another brain surgery. His infection responds to the antibiotics, but he's still exhausted.

"You staying tonight?" Mason's nurse Katie asks me.

"No, I have to get some sleep," I say. "My number is on the whiteboard. The hotel is right across the street. I can be back in five minutes if you need me."

"I'll take care of him for you," Katie says. "Go, sleep."

I kiss Mason's forehead and grab my purse.

I worry that Katie sees me as a bad mother, a selfish person. It's going on eleven p.m. I need to lie flat in a bed without anyone waking me up every hour when they flash penlights in Mason's eyes, without the beeping of the monitors and the buzz of the alarms. It's a desperate, hardwired need that I can't ignore another night.

I go and pass the night in a dead sleep of necessity.

I wake up to a text from Alan. He's arrived at the hospital directly from the airport. All is well. I stay behind and do a load of laundry and a half hour on the stationary bike in the gym.

My friends remind me that I need to take care of myself, that I can't give Mason what I don't have. I must sleep, eat, and get some exercise. So I push aside the old idea that it's selfish to take care of me in times of crisis. Mountain climbers say, "Climb high and sleep low." Even the toughest mountaineers acknowledge the need to recuperate when ascending atypical heights. I've been living in a high-pressure, low-oxygen zone for months now, determined to use the force of my mind to overrule the needs of my body—as if I could exist on worry and list-making.

I need oxygen. I've been holding my breath until I know that everything turns out okay so I can live my life again. But I seem to be destined to live with only as much reassurance as I can squeeze out of any given moment. Right now is all I have. I've been hunkering down, getting through, waiting until the crisis passes to have a life I recognize. But this is it—the life I've got.

I can't give my family what I don't have. Self-care was the first thing to go. It's that intrinsic inner kindness, the instinctive infant state that tells us to eat when hungry, sleep when tired, and love without question or condition.

"I guess nobody is going to do it for me," I tell my friend Julie.

"Nobody can," she reminds me.

I start a new routine. While Mason dozes during his liquid lunch, I walk through the tree-lined neighborhood just outside the medical center. A man watering his drooping petunias looks at me suspiciously because people in Houston know better than to walk in the heat of the day. But the slap of the hot air outside the hospital doors feels good. I peel off my sweater. There's reassurance in seeing the neatly clipped lawns, cats dozing on cool cement stoops, the red-brick houses. There's a world oblivious to our crisis, unbroken, peaceful, and predictable.

It helps to know it's nearby.

# twenty-six

# It's Not About the Haircut

*It turns out we came to Texas for proton therapy. Who knew?* I write on Mason's CaringBridge, a website where friends can track what's going on. Alan has been a much more prolific contributor, posting cheerful progress reports whenever he's here. Me, I don't write that much. I have a hard time capturing the right tone, cheerful but not dishonest, realistic but not morose.

We surrender to the care of Texas Children's Hospital, and there is great relief in this. The team offers Mason a full inpatient rehab program while he gets proton treatment. Mason's radiation oncologist is calm and smart. She's not particularly awed by Mason's tumor, and she seems to believe me when I tell her he was once a good student who could also walk, talk, and eat just fine.

I decide this is a God Thing, the confluence of circumstance that got us to this team of doctors and this method of treatment at this moment in time. Faith seems to mean seeing good in the places I don't want to be. It's the evidence that Joan talked about. Some days I have to look really hard. But even the Dodger-fan doctor brings with him a certain kind of grace because no matter how tired Mason is, when Dodger doctor scoffs at the Giant's pennant taped to the wall, Mason musters the words "Go, Giants," or if he's really feeling it, "Dodgers suck."

*Thank you*, I whisper whenever I remember.

Now that we've committed to another six weeks in Houston, we find a short-term rental with two bedrooms and a kitchen with a refrigerator that will fit more than a yogurt and a half pint of milk.

My mom arrives in time for Mason's first proton session. His face is still mostly frozen, but a smile has begun to animate his features. She sits next to Mason's bed, massaging the tension out of his tight-fisted right hand.

"Mason, I'm keeping my Christmas tree up until you can come over and open your presents," Mom says. "Believe me, it's going to be worth your while."

A slow curve moves up the left side of Mason's mouth.

"Yes!" Mason says. The word comes quick with some force behind it.

"Wow, Mason you are getting so much better," Mom says, tears in her eyes.

I nod. I can't hear it enough. I'm so aware of how far we have to go, it's easy to lose track of how far we've come since Mason couldn't sit upright or form words when we left California. Now that his shunt is fixed, he's more present behind his eyes, able to engage and focus when in therapy.

Two paramedics appear in the doorway with a gurney. "Ready to head to the proton center, Mason?" the taller one asks.

I don't love the idea of radiating my son's brain. Alan and I both signed the consent form, although only one signature was required. Once again, we were treated to a laundry list of potential consequences: memory loss, speech impairment, hair loss, secondary cancers. As always, we weigh these dangers against the risk of doing nothing.

We pray, and the answer comes. There is a quiet but steady, directional pull. Alan feels it too. It's the right decision. I sense it in the pit of myself, but it's still hard to follow Mason's gurney through the doors of the proton radiation center. We pass a brass gong in the hallway.

"You ring the gong when you have your last treatment," the nurse explains.

Aerosmith is blasting in the treatment room, an oddly perfect soundtrack. It's like a weird sci-fi nightclub.

"Wow, Mason, this is so cool," I force myself to say. "It looks like something out of *Star Wars*, doesn't it?"

The entire back wall is taken up by the proton machine. In the center of the room is what looks like a giant ray gun whose beam will shoot through my thirteen-year-old son's skull while he lies on the table positioned below it.

Mason smiles, a faint one-sided grin. He doesn't seem scared.

"All right, Mason," Mark, the radiation tech, explains. "This won't hurt at all. The only thing you need to do is stay very still."

Mark fixes a custom-made plastic mask over Mason's face, securing it to the table so he can't move and the radiation will hit exactly the right spot.

One treatment down, twenty-four to go.

---

A few weeks into proton therapy, Mason's hair begins to fall out on the left side, turning his white pillowcase furry brown. A kidney-bean-shaped bald spot is emerging. His hair is three different lengths where it's been cut for various surgeries over the past four months.

"Let's get Mason's hair cut tonight," Alan says in front of his mother, Janice, who arrived the day after my mom left. There's a barber who visits the hospital every week. All we have to do is wheel Mason up to the recreation floor for a free haircut.

"That's not going to happen," I say with some force. "Looking weird isn't worth risking a scrape or a cut that would prohibit him from getting his proton therapy."

I feel real panic, like Alan's proposing giving a gang of eighth-grade bullies razor blades and setting them lose on my son's scalp. I know it's not logical. A knot forms in my belly. I'm a people pleaser, except with Alan, of course. Now Janice gets to watch me argue with her perfect son.

"The doctor said it's okay," Alan says in his CEO voice.

"It's not okay with me," I say in my mom voice.

Janice doesn't say a word, at least not until I leave.

---

I'd like an off switch.

Drinking did this for me briefly until my dad ruined it by getting sober. I was a senior in college when he took me out for a nice dinner and introduced me to the idea that my solution might become my problem.

The waiter presented Dad with his Diet Coke and me with a fishbowl of the prettiest blush-colored wine. I'd just turned twenty-one, after all. I cringed when I realized that it might not be good form to drink wine in front of one's newly sober father.

"It's okay," Dad said, taking a long drag from his straw.

"You know, if you were an alcoholic, you'd have to finish that whole glass," he explained, buttering a slice of sourdough. "An alcoholic is powerless."

Alarmed, I decided right then to finish half the glass to reassure him (and me) that I wasn't an alcoholic.

"Turns out there are a lot of sober guys in town," Dad went on. "Good people too. I've got some new friends."

I nodded. I smiled. I gauged the halfway mark on my fishbowl.

I didn't mention the strange experience I had after a lingering Happy Hour at a Mexican restaurant when I picked up the phone in my apartment and there was no dial tone, only Spanish music. When I asked my neighbor about it, he looked at me like I was crazy, when he was the forty-year-old guy who spent his days surfing and his nights emptying the Corona bottles that overflowed from the recycling bin. Weird.

I took another polite sip.

"So there's this genetic component to alcoholism," Dad said. "You might want to just keep an eye on it as you get older. Not that you have a problem."

He wasn't pretending, and neither was I. I had all the signs of *not* being an alcoholic (except what happened sometimes when I drank). We finished our grilled mahi-mahi around the time I'd consumed exactly half the wine. Dad pulled out his American Express. I took another big sip while he calculated the tip because you're not an alcoholic if you leave a half glass of wine behind. And who's to know if it's just a little less than half?

I'm sober twenty-two years now, and I don't think about drinking, not seriously. It's like noticing the man in the elevator has nice lips. It's not like I'm going to do anything about it. This, I concede, is a miracle. But once in a while, in between me and that miracle, a space opens up that is vulnerable to tides of ingratitude, worry, and all-consuming terror. There are moments when it's just me, the abyss, and a God with whom I've decided to play hide-and-seek. At these times, it all feels too hard.

I call my friend Cynthia on my afternoon walk through my favorite Houston neighborhood and tell her about Alan's horrible haircut idea. She, too, is married a long time.

"Compassion for you. Compassion for Alan," she says. "Have you taken any time to meditate? Just ten minutes?"

She's one of those people who believes that the solution has nothing to do with the problem. I was looking forward to discussing how angry I am—and justified—but maybe she has a point. Compassion for Alan might be noticing the hurt in his eyes. Could seeing Mason's messy hair be a painful reminder of every surgery, every scare? Everything we couldn't protect him from? How far away we are from normal?

I win this round. Mason won't have his hair cut for a long time. Alan flies home and writes a glowing post on Mason's CaringBridge site, praising Mason's "magnificent mom," which is sweet, though slightly baffling.

Compassion for me might be acknowledging that I'm grabbing for anything I can control in Mason's hospital room, and there's not much.

# twenty-seven

# The Weight of Air

Two weeks later I take my turn going home to California. I pick up Sarah at school in the car Alan left at the airport when he flew to Houston. We're achieving a freaky efficiency in our hand-offs.

While I'm parked in front of the school, it occurs to me there might be a sixteen-week-old peanut butter sandwich in Mason's locker. Reluctantly I head toward the front steps.

A few mothers I don't recognize lean against the fence. They nod when I walk by as if I hadn't spent last night piecing together a jigsaw puzzle in the proton center. They don't know me. They don't know my story. It's a relief to pass as a normal mom.

I find Mason's locker covered with messages scribbled in dry-erase markers. "We love you, Mason." "Come Back Soon." "Miss you." There's no decomposing peanut butter, just heartfelt graffiti.

Sarah walks toward me and notices my eyes welling up. Before she has a chance to comment on how embarrassing it is to find your mother crying in your school hallway, she sighs. "I don't feel very good."

"We're going to have a quiet weekend," I say, putting an arm around her.

She's probably just tired. Sarah can't be sick because I can't get sick. That would mean I can't be at the hospital or the radiation center with Mason.

At home the house smells a little more like dog than I remember. The animals circle. Moseley, the Golden Retriever, is grayer. Jesse, the rescue mutt, is skinnier. I fix Sarah an Airborne and hand her the fizzling glass. We settle into my king-sized bed, watching *Modern Family* on the DVR. Austin is at baseball practice. Sarah falls asleep immediately, snuggled into the crook of my arm. I kiss her damp, pink face and notice she's definitely feverish. But I'm not going to let her go.

I smell her hair, a mix between lily-of-the-valley shampoo and a ten-year-old who spent fifth period playing kickball.

I pull her closer and close my eyes.

---

Mason has eighteen sessions to go when an early appointment opens up at the proton center. This allows Alan and me to have dinner at a relatively normal time. The food is one of my favorite things about Houston, along with gospel rap, which I didn't even know existed until I'd flipped through local radio. Alan and I sit at a restaurant table, not talking much. I order chicken enchiladas. Alan digs into his green chile rellenos.

"You could have returned my call today," he says.

"I'm sorry; I forgot to charge my phone."

"Even when your phone is working, you don't always pick up when I call," he complains.

My stomach tenses, predicting the gathering storm. This is an old argument. When Alan calls, he expects me to make myself available, no matter what's going on. He says he always picks up when I call though I'm not sure that's entirely true.

"There are women in this world who are happy when I call," he says.

I don't toss the enchiladas at him, but I consider it. "Who are you talking about?" I hiss. "Do these hypothetical women have thirteen-year-olds in the hospital getting their brains irradiated?"

I'm sure the "happy when I call" women didn't hear him yelling at a nurse, which he did yesterday. But my not answering might have more to do with not wanting to hear from anyone with suggestions, needs, or opinions—especially four months into this torture cycle of little sleep, high stress, and, oh yeah, being removed from the people and places that anchor me and remind me who I am.

Each new nurse refers to me as "Mom." As in "Mom, did you notice this rash yesterday?" "Mom, does Mason have any allergies to medication?" It's sweet, preferable to the nurses calling out, "Hey, you." And it's a fact of this existence that "Janine" is getting pushed further away. I'm a little lost, lonely, and, right now, desperate.

"Who is this woman who's happy to hear from you?" My voice rises along with my blood pressure.

Alan obviously still has a life outside of the seventh floor of the children's hospital, working with attractive women who work out regularly and get their rays from the sun rather than hospital fluorescent bulbs. I take inventory of my own appearance. My hair is limp and losing color faster than my pale skin. I've been washing with hospital soap for months now, and my hands have taken on a desert tortoise quality. Manicures consist of nibbling the rough edges off my cuticles.

"It's not like that. It's just . . . I need more," he says, combining a complaint and a demand into three short words.

I stare at my husband disbelievingly. Is he insane? How could he expect any more from me right now?

"I'm doing the best I can. It's all about Mason right now," I say carefully.

"So am I. And I have to work too."

"What do you think I do all day? Sit around reading magazines?" I shove my enchiladas away from me, hard. I glare at him. "Who is she?" I demand.

Alan leans back, watching me blow up from the grenade he's tossed, the one I've caught and swallowed. His eyes narrow into an icy green.

"I'm speaking in general," he says calmly, as if I'm the one with the problem.

My vision blurs with tears. This stranger across from me is Alan: my steady, reliable, once-madly-in-love-with-me husband. Who is he? Who are we? I didn't expect Alan to give up on us. Not now, in the middle of the crisis that keeps stretching deeper and longer.

Alan throws down his credit card. I can't sit at the table for one more minute. I head for the van. A few minutes later Alan gets into the driver's seat. We sit like sculptures, staring at the cement wall in front of us. Even though Alan is the most annoying person in my life right now, I feel that clench, the grip of fear. I don't want to lose him or our family. And despite scream-singing Adele's "We Could Have Had It All" on continuous loop when I'm alone in the minivan, I'm not sure I could survive a divorce. I am barely getting through as it is.

"I do love you," he says. "That's never the problem."

"I love you too," I say. "I'm sorry."

I didn't think the annoyance I felt when I saw Alan's name on my incoming calls had been obvious. I don't want to do this alone, but I also want to do it entirely my way. Alan's input, unless it is directly in line with mine, feels like criticism. I appreciate how hard he works, the paychecks that pay for these dinners out, the apartment, and, of course, always topping my gratitude list, our health insurance. It was thoughtless for him to press the "she" button like he did but maybe not. Maybe he knew the reaction he'd get, and he wanted connection at any cost. I know about unskillful, sleep-deprived, adrenaline-intoxicated sharp shooting. I tend to excuse it in myself. From him, not so much.

I lock eyes with my husband. He's crying too.

"This is just so hard," he says, swiping tears off his face.

"I need you," I say.

I can't remember the last time I touched down on any need inside myself. I can't afford to sink into the quicksand of buried needs that live in that dark, soundproof place. Alan puts his arms around me. We hug across the minivan console for a long time.

"We should get back before the night nurse arrives," he says, breaking the trance.

"Yeah," I say, wiping my eyes.

We look at each other. "You have something in your teeth," I say. Alan uses the hospital parking pass to pick out a peppercorn.

I need it to be okay between us. I am so wrung out. The tears relieve a pressure that's been building. I'm more scared than angry. Sure, it's hard between us, but underneath the annoyance, the distance, the disagreements, I've always been certain that we're in this together. I don't know how to live in a world where this isn't true.

On the walk across the lot into the hospital, Alan slips his hand in mine. It's the warm nights that I like the very best about Houston. The air has substance and weight, a presence of its own. This warmth infuses the silence between us right now, fortifying against the blast of AC that comes every time we step through the hospital door.

The next morning when I wake up and wander into the living room of our rented apartment, Alan looks up from his laptop.

"I'm going to work from Houston from now on," he says. "I let everyone know that I won't be in the office."

"Wow, are you sure?"

Alan nods. "What could be more important?"

I arrange myself in his lap. I vaguely remember this feeling, being close to my husband. There's a melting inside me where I've been hardening myself, making myself tough enough to manage being here mostly alone.

"Thank you," I say.

He pulls me close. There's a feeling like submerging in a hot bath, letting go, relief and a shadow of achiness where the clench used to be.

While Mason is between PT and speech therapy sessions, I drive to the market and buy a cart full of vegetables.

That night I return to our rented apartment where I chop yams, leeks, carrots, and red potatoes into rough-skinned chunks. I toss them into a large pot of water, along with garlic (antimicrobial/anticancer), sea salt (minerals), and a sheet of kombu seaweed (more minerals). This is "magic mineral broth," a recipe from a cancer cookbook that a friend gave me back in the "good old days," when all Mason had was a tumor that wasn't doing much of anything, back when I was explaining to anyone who would listen that some people live their entire lives with dull, plodding tumors in their heads.

The following day I strain the vegetables to make a clear golden broth that won't clog Mason's G-tube.

"Wait till you see what I've got for you," I tell Mason.

He looks at me bright-eyed, sitting upright in his hospital bed, wearing a pair of black basketball shorts and one of his Giants T-shirts.

I take the plastic feed bag down from the pole, fill it with a cup of broth, and hang it again. I set the pump to begin feeding my son and watch as the tubes fill golden orange.

"What's that?" asks Carla, Mason's nurse, when she brings his morning medication.

"It's this broth I made. It has a lot of minerals and different nutrients . . ."

"That's so cool," Carla says. "I love it."

Mason gives us that thirteen-year-old "Oh, Mom" expression, maybe even raising an eyebrow, which is its own kind of progress. But since he doesn't have to taste the broth, he doesn't protest. After a few days I notice he's taken on a faint soup-y aroma, which is better than the slightly sweet, metallic, nutrition-in-a-can body odor. It might be my imagination, but he seems to focus more in speech therapy, and his words sound a little clearer.

Alan calls from San Francisco, where he's putting in a busy week, tying up loose ends. I pick up his call on the second ring. I'm trying. I update him on Mason's therapies, including the broth project.

I position the day's activities through the half-full lens, which I figure is just as accurate as the opposite point of view. Mason has therapy three times a day and access to world-class cancer treatment. That's amazing. I'm pretending to be a positive, grateful person, hoping eventually I'll feel like one.

*twenty-eight*

# Don't Stop Believing

Mason and his physical therapist Dave return early from their afternoon stroll around the seventh floor. Mason is slumped over the walker. His eyes are glazed. Bored, sad, exhausted, it's hard to tell.

"He keeps yawning, and he doesn't seem to have the stamina to do more today," Dave explains. "We'll try again tomorrow." He unhooks Mason from the walker, then transfers him back to bed.

"Are you okay, Mace?" I ask.

Mason shakes his head, his mouth in a half-frown. He seems sad, fed up, and ready for all this to be over. This is my guess, but all these feelings must be compounded by his current inability to express them beyond a limited cache of facial expressions and even fewer words.

There was a time I could fix just about anything for my son. I was a full-service source of comfort, protection, and sustenance. These days I make the broth and sit vigil at his bedside, frustrated by my inability to do more. I chase away the coughing resident who insists she's "not contagious anymore," and then I borrow a tub of the

191

hospital's disinfecting wipes and clean the doorknobs and bed rails because I'd rather disinfect the windowsill than sit still. I do what I can, but I'd prefer the ability to give the tumor a stern talking to that would make it disappear; I'd like the strength to massage function back into Mason's dormant right hand and a touch that would relieve the fear and pain trapped behind his eyes. The limits of my abilities as Mason's mother (and a human being) are obvious, a fissure in the earth brought to the surface by a temblor of circumstance. Still, I try.

While Mason naps, I log on to iTunes. I have an idea. The next day, when Dave arrives for Mason's session, I'm ready. I press play on my iPod. "Eye of the Tiger" blasts into the room. Mason's eyes brighten while Dave straps him in the man-sized walker, ordered especially for my extra-large child.

In the corridor Mason takes big steps while I follow close behind, his iPod roadie. This is the fastest Mason has moved since before the bleed.

Next up on the "Motivate Mason Mixtape" is Journey's "Don't Stop Believing," a San Francisco Giants' theme song. Mason hunkers down. I can see it in his face, the will he's using to push the signals from his brain into his body to propel himself forward. We reach the first nurse's station.

A young woman in bright Garfield scrubs looks up and begins to clap. Mason takes another big step and another.

Mason pumps his left hand in the air, momentarily letting go of the walker. He doesn't seem to think about it. He raises a hand, then puts it right back on his walker.

"What do you think, Mason?" Dave asks. "Ready for a break?"

Mason shakes his head no.

The next song is Katy Perry's "California Gurls," a favorite from last summer.

Mason manages another full lap before it's all over. Dave unbuckles him and transfers him into his bed, and he falls into a deep sleep. We have two hours until proton tonight. I use the time to add to the playlist. A feeling I vaguely remember as joy slices through the dull ache that I now realize is not an essential part of me.

———

While Alan wraps things up in San Francisco, my friend Joan comes to visit. Mason has just finished lunch when she wheels her suitcase into the room.

"Mason, how are you?" she asks. "You're looking so much better than the last time I saw you!"

"I'm gooood," he says, drawing out his description for maximum effect.

"You're just in time for his PT," I say. "Wait until you see him do laps around the hospital."

Dan arrives and straps Mason into the man-sized walker, then Joan and I follow them into the hall, and I turn on the playlist. Today it's the *Rocky* theme song. Mason takes one long step, then another, looking over his shoulder at Joan, who's clapping madly.

"Mason, do you want to give your friend a ride?" Dan asks. Then to Joan, "Are you up for it?"

He holds her hand while she steps onto the back of the walker, gripping the metal frame.

"Let's go," Joan says.

Mason grins and makes two more laps around the hospital floor with my seventy-seven-year-old, eighty-five-pound friend perched on the back of his walker.

Afterward, with Mason settled into his bed, Joan pulls her chair up next to him.

"Ouch!" Mason yells.

Joan jumps.

"What happened?" I ask.

Then I notice Mason's face. He's watching us with a broad—almost symmetrical—smile.

"Ouch," he says again, and we get it. He's messing with us.

"Oh, Mason, you trickster." Joan laughs.

"What?" he teases.

---

That night at the apartment Joan and I sit side by side in our pajamas. She puts her arm around me. I rest my head on her shoulder. "It's okay," she says. "Just let go."

"I don't know how," I say.

"It's okay," she repeats. "Breathe."

I manage a contracted breath that ends near my sternum. Joan doesn't relax her firm grip on me.

"I'm here. It's okay, Janine," she says. "Just breathe."

I surrender to her bear hug because she won't let me go until I do. She's bony but surprisingly strong. I push through brittle layers of embarrassment, and then I begin to cry as if I'll never stop.

---

Alan returns to Houston, and we slip into an easy routine where he works in the morning and meets me at the hospital in the afternoon. We have dinner together most nights before Mason's proton session.

"Los Lonely Boys is playing at House of Blues tonight. Any chance I can take you there for a late birthday celebration?" Alan asks across Mason's bed.

The word *no* reflexively forms in my mouth, but this time I stifle it.

"That could be nice," I say instead. It would be nice to be the sort of person who goes to clubs and listens to music.

I run my fingers through my hair, nibble the rough edge off a fingernail. Had I known I was going out, I would've worn a different T-shirt and maybe a pair of flats instead of sneakers.

At House of Blues, Alan takes my hand and cuts through the crowd with ease, a talent he acquired at the hundreds of Grateful Dead shows he's attended. We aim toward the stage under flashing lights, purple, red, and green.

The band has a certain ease and exuberance that moves the people in the room, including me. We sway like a tide. A woman in red cowboy boots smiles as we pass. She has polished nails and expensive highlights. The guy she's with takes a pull from his Budweiser.

The music shakes something loose in me. Alan puts his arm around me, and we move together.

When I *think* about us, I flip through the index of things said, feelings hurt. The misdeeds float to the top of the stack. I'm a score-keeper, which has something to do with protecting myself, but also a pathological need to be right. I gird against caring as much as I do. I gird against the loss of who we were and the blank space of who we are becoming.

But it's too loud to think. The only thing to do is move to the music and sing out loud. I forget to be afraid.

"Y'all ready for one more song?" one of the Garza brothers yells from the stage.

The crowd roars.

I wish I had some cowboy boots.

---

As soon as school is out for the summer, Austin and Sarah fly to Houston so we can bring Mason home as a family. When I imagined this day, I saw Mason walking onto the plane and stashing his backpack in the overhead compartment. Now I realize he won't be cured before we leave. He's better. He speaks in three-word sentences, at least until he's tired and goes back to nodding his head. The trach is gone. He can stand up, if he's supported, but he can't take more than one or two steps on his own.

Our favorite ambulance crew picks us up for Mason's last proton session. I suspect Mason has a crush on Robin, the young EMT with brown eyes and a thick ponytail. She cranks the gurney up to the height of the ambulance and slides him inside.

Robin smiles and pulls a Houston Astros hat out of her bag.

"Go, Giants." Mason laughs.

"This is so you remember us," Robin says, and slips the hat onto his head.

"It's your last proton session," I remind him. "You get to go home in two days."

I repeat the countdown because Mason's eyes widen with surprise every time I do. His radiation oncologist reassures us that short-term memory loss is to be expected and will likely heal over time.

This morning, Alan wheeled Mason around in his wheelchair with a box of cupcakes on his lap so he could hand them out to the nurses.

"Thank you, thank you, thank you." It's all we could say. Words aren't big enough to hold this gratitude. Mason won't remember celebrating his fourteenth birthday in the hospital, but I will. The way the nurses and aides hung banners and streamers. The parade of well-wishers making an ordinary hospital day into something like a party.

After his final half hour in the proton machine, our family plus the EMTs meet Mason near the treatment room. The radiation tech hands Mason a wooden mallet. He looks at the stick in his hand, baffled, that hole in his short-term memory gaping.

"It's your last proton session. You get to bang the gong," I remind him.

Mason's eyes shine.

"We get to go home now!" Alan reminds him.

Robin raises the gurney to a seated position and wheels Mason up to the gong. Mason knits his brow and puts all of his energy into the swing. The sound reverberates through each and every one of us. We cheer together.

I feel relieved and terrified. We don't know what's next. We'll watch the tumor on Mason's MRIs and hope it will shrink and not grow. We hope it will no longer bleed.

*The tumor's dead*, I tell myself, deciding to believe it's true.

# twenty-nine

# Mortals Like Us

Bringing Mason home is like bringing home a newborn, minus the milk-filled breasts that can fix most anything. There's no manual for what to do when this human is six feet tall and unable to walk, bathe, and eat on his own.

I'm lying in bed next to Mason, staring at my very own ceiling. I put a hand on his chest to measure his breathing. I'll sleep beside him until I'm sure he can make it through the night on his own. I'm happy to be back with my kids, my friends, and my weedy garden.

A new level of work begins now. It's not up to an institution, the doctor, or the therapists (though they'll have big roles). It's up to me to pull all these pieces together and bring Mason fully back into himself. I believe that God is ultimately in charge of this process. But I also know that God gave me skills, and I'm sure we both want the same thing—for Mason to be back where he was before, walking, talking, eating, and going to college someday.

A slight whistle comes through the hole in Mason's neck where his trach used to be. The opening was supposed to close by itself, and it mostly did, but there's still a tiny black hole. It's another surgery we'll have to deal with sometime, but it's not urgent.

There's no night nurse to look after Mason. There's me, making sure he doesn't wake up and forget that he can't walk, that he doesn't fall or roll onto the floor. I notice a rip in the heart of myself, lying next to my fourteen-year-old son who can't get up to go to the bathroom on his own, but I don't dare pull on the threads. I don't cry. I refuse to get depressed or overwhelmed. Feelings like these are for people who don't have such elaborate to-do lists.

I ignore the thick vein of fear (*What if he doesn't get any better?*) because it's disloyal to think that way. Instead, I focus on what I need to do so this life tips toward a miracle. I pray too. Of course I do. It's on the list.

We hire an in-home rehabilitation company so that we don't have to repeat the considerable effort to get Mason in and out of the car several times a day. On our first Monday at home, Rachael, Mason's new physical therapist, teaches him to use a walker. It's a regular walker, not like the one at the hospital that supported him with a safety harness.

Mason's legs get tangled up. But he persists, pushing the walker the length of our family room before exhaustion lands him back in his wheelchair.

"What's that?" Sarah asks when Rachael leaves, pointing to the aluminum contraption.

"It's to help Mason walk until he can balance by himself."

"It's like for an old person," Sarah says. "It's ugly. Can I fix it up?"

I nod.

Mason dozes in his wheelchair. He doesn't seem to care how his walker looks. And if he does care, he can't say.

I go upstairs to roast a chicken for dinner. I'll make bone broth from the carcass, nutrition-rich and healing. I'm moving forward the same way Mason is: left foot, right foot, sleepwalking through this odd new reality. But at least I know these halls, this stairway, the path to the refrigerator.

When I come back downstairs, Sarah shows me that she's wrapped Mason's walker in orange and black duct tape, candy-cane style.

Mason smiles when he sees it. Sarah turns the TV to *I Love Lucy*, a show they both like. I fill a clean plastic feed bag with coconut water, hang it from my very own steel pole, and attach the tubes to Mason's G-tube.

This is how we arrive in that long summer, the first season in our new reality.

———

Mason works out with the dedication of a body builder, only the muscles he's building are the invisible, taken-for-granted ones deep inside. Four weeks into home therapy, Mason's core still lacks the strength to hold him upright for longer than twenty minutes. It's a grueling process, but his young body is responsive. Progress is measured in minutes, which accumulate into milestones.

One Thursday Rachael announces that we're going to take Mason downtown to practice using the walker. I match her brightly lit enthusiasm with something close to dread. There are curbs downtown, also dogs, cracked sidewalks, and bicycles. Maneuvering Mason into the car requires activation of hibernating, yawning muscles not eager to engage. I trust Rachael, but there are also people downtown, and in Mason's present state, with the infant gaze on his teenage face, he seems too vulnerable to withstand their scrutiny.

Really, I'm the unsteady one, not sure how to handle the stares of strangers that remind me how banged up Mason actually is. I'm almost getting used to the placid expression on his face. It's getting harder to remember what he looked like before, the memories becoming still photographs in my mind. But I rally because it's progress, uncomfortable and scary progress.

"Okay," Mason musters a word and a confident nod.

We park in front of the hardware store where Rachael takes the walker from the trunk and transfers Mason out of the car with a graceful PT "one, two." He stands hunched behind the brightly decorated old man's walker. But he's standing. Then he's walking, one, two, pause, one, two, pause. I follow behind, pushing the wheelchair in case he needs it. I nod to the people who pass our procession. I wipe a tear that slips down under my sunglasses. *It's going to be okay*, I say with my achy smile.

I worry about Austin and Sarah when I'm not obsessing about Mason falling, going into a seizure, or having another bleed. I missed the entire spring semester of Austin's sophomore year, a season of basketball games, English papers to proofread, curfews to enforce, and hugs to administer at the end of the night. Sarah grew three inches while I was away. She acquired a new best friend and a penchant for pedicures along with a frequent craving for brownies with whipped cream.

My original plan was that these children have no hardship. This would likely mean that they'd come out of my house with as much depth as a Hershey bar (sweet, thin, and vulnerable to heat), but I figured they could learn empathy at a safe distance from actual terrifying circumstances. The universe seems to have a more hands-on approach in mind.

Sarah clears the line to Mason's G-tube bag when a clog sets off an alarm. Austin fetches the remote and negotiates a settlement when the three of them can't agree on what to watch on TV. They are appropriately cranky, meaning they aren't pitying or condescending. Mason is still the annoying little/big brother, and they're in this together, all three of them.

Austin is now seventeen, and one of the most capable people I know, with his twelve-year-old sister showing commensurate skill. Still, I worry about putting too much responsibility on either one of them.

"Are you okay staying with Mason while I get some groceries?" I ask Austin. "Either that or you could go. I can give you a list."

"Go," he says. "We're fine."

Thank God. I need to get out of the house. I need to listen to the radio in the car, loud. I need to browse the body-care section of the grocery store and try some new face lotion because it appears I've been aging in dog years.

Thirty minutes later, remarkably refreshed, I stumble through the front door with four bags of groceries. "How'd it go?"

"He had a little accident," Austin says. "But I took care of it."

There's an empty cup, a wet rag in the corner, drops of juice dotting the wall. "He tried to get up by himself," Austin says. "He knocked over the table."

"Thanks for handling that," I say, noticing Mason is wearing a fresh T-shirt and shorts. "You changed his clothes too?" I ask Austin, amazed.

"And he needed a shower." Austin shrugs. "No big deal."

Mason looks up from his sketchbook and shrugs too. He is gripping a pen in his left hand. He has begun to fill pages with fine-lined drawings. Tiny triangles, squares, and arrows form bigger patterns and fill the pages. Of feelings? Of the words that can't find their way out of his mouth?

His sketchbooks are a clue that there is a lot going on inside that he can't express through facial expressions and his small cadre of words. He fills two hundred blank pages in two weeks. I buy him another book, then another.

When Mason's occupational therapist Kate arrives one Wednesday, Sarah is pinning a polka-dotted jersey to her dress mannequin to create a new top. I'm vacuuming up dog hair from the corners of the room so that Kate doesn't report me to CPS.

"Can I get you a glass of water?" I ask as she settles in with her basket of props: balls, cards, a soup can of pennies taped shut with duct tape.

"I'm fine," she says. "Mason, are you ready to get to work?"

He nods.

"What was that?" I face him with my eyes closed. This is meant to discourage him from using gestures to communicate and encourage him to practice his words. I have become even more annoying than I used to be.

"Okay." He sighs, and I'm sure he would roll his eyes if he could.

I retreat to the kitchen to clean up the detritus of breakfast, a virtual crime scene of egg yolks and toast crumbs.

"Ouch!" Mason yells.

I take the stairs two at a time.

Kate is sitting across from Mason in the "hands up" position. Her silver eyebrows high.

"I don't know what happened. I just tossed him the ball, and he yelled out," she says.

I notice a smile has animated the left side of Mason's face.

Sarah shakes her head. "Mason," she says. "It's not funny."

I shoot him the knock-it-off look.

"He's joking," I say. "I'm sure you didn't do anything."

Kate takes a deep, cleansing breath. "You got me," she says.

"It's his sense of humor," I explain. "He's always been like that."

It's my mission to make sure no one thinks that Mason is any less himself now than he was before. It's an absolute necessity that we (all the people in the world) believe that full recovery isn't just possible but inevitable.

"You can't do that," I tell Mason after Kate leaves. "People will think you're not all here, and you are. You really are."

Mason smiles and shakes his head.

I thought being home would be easier. That I would fold myself back into my life. But it seems that I now have an "old life" and whatever this is now. The bones of me seem to have been rearranged. I, too, struggle to find my balance.

Annie doesn't let this deter her. There's a meditation group she's been wanting to try, and I am eager to get out of the house. We arrive at the community center, and I recognize a woman named Josephine.

"I don't think I've seen you here before," she says.

"First time," I say. "My friend wanted to try it, and I tagged along."

She gives me "the look," the one I've come to recognize—that of pity and relief that she's not me.

"Well, I think it could be very helpful," she says meaningfully. "How *is* Mason?"

"Good," I say. "He's working really hard in therapy. He'll start back in school next week."

She takes my hand, though I don't offer it. "What is his prognosis?"

Is she really asking me if Mason will die?

"Mortal, same as you and me," I say, oddly upbeat.

I find Annie in the corner of the room where she's saved a spot for me.

I whisper, "I've been bad."

"Just in the last five minutes?"

I nod grimly. "Someone gave me the look. I was snarky."

She smiles. "Atta girl."

My filter isn't what it used to be.

It's not easy being me right now, not that it ever was. It's just that before, I had more of a reliable candy shell between me and the world. Now I feel oddly exposed, also exhausted and grumpy. Every bit of me, every shred of energy goes into managing this life of ours. I still believe that if I can get it right, our storyline might tip toward acceptable, even great. Growing up with unpredictable people, the challenge was to wrestle circumstances into submission. We pretended to trust God, especially on Sunday mornings. Though we secretly hoped He wasn't paying too close attention on Friday and Saturday nights.

There's no drinking in our home these days, but we bring a subtle form of what's called "the family disease of alcoholism," a tangle of fishing line that trips us into believing that our problems lie outside of ourselves. We'll be happier "when" or "if." It's almost logical and sane in our present situation. We'll be okay once Mason is okay. We'll have our lives back when he does, but really the days keep ticking away.

I'm steeped in circumstances I can't seem to master. I can't control the tumor any more than I could control my father's drinking or ultimately my own. I understand this now.

But how do I bring Mason back to the life he's supposed to have? How do I make sure my other kids aren't damaged by this experience? How do I convince Alan to support my vision for all things family related?

How do I summon superhuman strength and God-like power as a mortal mother of three?

# thirty

# The Other Track

ˇ

Mason has no social life. Alan thinks we should invite his friends over. I agree though I'm still afraid of them seeing Mason in this nakedness, so raw and different from the boy he was before. Bumping into them for a quick hello out in the world is one thing. But if they sit here too long, they'll figure out that Mason can't really talk right now, not more than two or three words in a row.

I don't have it in me to persuade them that Mason is still here, just quieter. Also, I know that kids instinctively see the truth, and I'm afraid of the truth they might see. But for the greater good, I muster enthusiasm I don't feel. These are the kids who sent a T-shirt from the class trip, mailed handmade cards, and wrote encouraging graffiti on his locker. I hug each of the boys and girls at the door, glad to see them, nervous about how the visit will go.

"Come in!" I say in an unfamiliar, cheerful voice. "I have lots of snacks."

They look much older than they did the last time I saw them, the girls now committed to their eyeliner. Some of the boys need a shave. They hurry past me to Mason, who's sitting in the family room recliner.

"You look great!" says JL.

Mason struggles. "Thanks," he says finally. His voice is monotone, and his smile is genuine.

If the kids are shocked by how different Mason looks—so much younger, slightly lost—they don't say so.

"How was Texas?" asks Odysseus.

Mason nods, as if to say, Texas was good. His face defaults back into his now typical half-smile.

⸺

I fumble with chips and guacamole. "Does anyone want a juice? Water? Brownies?" I hover because it's what I do. Worry is my superpower. My friend Cynthia says worry is a form of control, or at least an illusion of it. I'm not sure she understands that my purpose in life is to think two steps ahead in order to anticipate and avoid trouble. What if Mason has to go to the bathroom? What if he forgets he can't stand up on his own?

Finally I back out of the room, busying myself in the kitchen. Then I realize that the sounds from the family room have stopped. Panicked, I run down the stairs. The room is empty. Where are they? Mason's walker is in the corner. I hear sounds from outside. They've moved to the backyard. *But he can't . . .*

"Mason!" I call from the doorway, holding his walker.

The kids are headed toward the picnic benches under the redwood trees, Mason trailing the pack. He has one arm around one of his friends and the other around another, both of whom happen to be girls with silky, long hair down their backs.

Mason looks over his shoulder at me, and with clear eyes, he shakes his head no.

In September, when Mason starts eighth grade for the second time, he's graduated from the walker to a cane, also decorated by Sarah with orange and black duct tape. His speech is limited, still hard to understand, but he's mostly eating on his own. The feeding tube will be removed in a few weeks.

"I'll see JL and Odysseus," Mason says as we load his backpack for the first day. Listening to him requires patience, fighting the impulse to finish his sentences—along with the impulse to protect him from all emotional and psychic pain.

"Sweetie, remember they graduated while you were in the hospital," I say. We've had this conversation several times thanks to Mason's short-term memory loss. "You'll be with Mr. D. and Miss Gough, and the kids who were in seventh grade last year."

"The little kids." Mason sighs dramatically.

Ashleigh has agreed to be Mason's helper, walking him from one class to the next to make sure he knows where he's going, taking notes in class for him, and unziplocking his sandwich at lunch.

"The little kids" welcome Mason warmly when he walks into homeroom. He's sort of a legend: the kid with a brain tumor who spent most of the last school year in the hospital, who's learning to walk and talk and be an eighth-grader all over again.

Mason continues his therapies. The goal, always, is to make him more independent, to be able to shower by himself, to go to school on his own.

My job is to find the best therapists and tutors, to keep everyone happy and moving through this uncomfortable in-between stage as quickly as possible. I want the new normal to be like the old normal. I want not to worry. I want Mason to catch up to his friends.

Alan is constantly working to secure a future for our highly insecure family. He is gone more than ever, trying to make up for lost time at work, those meetings and deals postponed. It's all happening now. I am grateful, and a little lonely. But it's still not my turn to have needs.

On the upside, after six months away, home is luscious. I lie in my bed with everyone safe under one roof, the cat sharing my pillow, and I'm okay. We're all okay; right now, right here.

---

With Mason beginning his final year of middle school, it's time to think about what comes next. The principal of Austin's small high school e-mailed me offering "anything you need." I ask for help brainstorming high school options for Mason, and Charles offers to meet with me.

"How's Mason?" Charles leans in as if we're already friends.

"He's doing really well back in school. Getting *A*s with some accommodations. We're in a difficult position because it's time to apply to schools, and it's hard for people who didn't know him before to understand who he is."

Charles nods.

"His speech is still affected, but it's getting better. His teachers love him. He can't always summon the right word immediately, but the neurologist says his cognitive abilities are still there. There's no reason he can't do well in high school."

I don't ask Charles to consider Mason for this beautiful school. I want it to be his idea.

"What if high school took six years?" he asks.

"That would be fine," I say too fast and too eager. "I'm in no hurry for him to go away to college."

"Do you think he could take Spanish?" Charles asks.

His question is based on graduation requirements for this school, and I'm ready for it.

"Mason's neurosurgeon says he could have a real aptitude for language right now, while he's rebuilding neural pathways."

Charles nods thoughtfully. "Let me get back to you after Thanksgiving," he says.

I take this to mean that he's going to talk to the relevant people and put together a six-year program for Mason, but he didn't actually say this.

I leave his office elated, certain that we'll work this out. Mason's teachers will have time to give him the attention he needs. He'll catch up to his friends, who already roam these bright hallways leaving their backpacks wherever they drop them without worrying they'll disappear.

Thanksgiving comes and goes. Charles doesn't call.

Christmas comes and goes. Charles doesn't call.

In January, I call him and set up another meeting.

Facing Charles across his desk, my smile is stiff. I'm praying furiously for God to make this happen—now. I'm certain that Mason should go to this school. I'm sure this idea of mine is, in fact, divinely inspired. Mason's classmates and teachers will rally around him. He'll be safe and nurtured, all the while gaining back the abilities he lost. It's the perfect setting.

"So," Charles asks after an awkward silence, "what are you thinking about high school for Mason?"

"He wants to come here," I sputter. So much for subtlety.

Charles frowns. "What's the status of his tumor?"

"It was treated with proton radiation," I explain, feeling like a saleswoman for the technology.

Charles straightens in his chair. "High school is a time when critical thinking skills come on board. And we don't know if Mason has those abilities."

My jaw is now in my lap. But I lock down my anger because Charles has to understand that I am right, and he has to want to help us.

"Cognitively, Mason is all there," I say. "He got an A on his Steinbeck paper. He's doing his algebra homework by himself. His speech is a problem, not his thinking. And his therapist says his speech should be in the normal range by September."

I push out of my mind how I had to keep reminding Mason who Lennie and George were when he narrated the Steinbeck paper while I typed. How every time I said, "Do you mean to say . . . ," or "What about . . . ," he nodded and slowly formed the word *yes*.

"The worst thing we can do is put Mason in a situation that sets him up to fail," Charles says.

"I won't let Mason fail." The words come out of me with force, my voice unrecognizable, louder and deeper. Doesn't he know that just nine months ago I wouldn't let him die?

"Isn't there a school for kids with brain injuries?" he asks. "What about boarding school?"

I take a sip of air through clenched teeth. It's difficult for me to go to the grocery store and leave him. I haven't gone to a movie in a year. Mason needs me. But I also need him. We all do.

I say in a jagged voice, "There aren't even many rehab facilities for kids with brain injuries. That's why our family spent four months in Houston, getting Mason the treatment he needed."

"I really wish you the best," Charles says, pushing back his chair to stand up.

I stare at him in disbelief, immobilized by the rage flaming through me that will soon rain down in a heavy ash of despair. I hold in the tears until I'm out of the building, in my car, driving away from this curated group of teenagers who play varsity sports as freshmen and restore habitats for endangered species on family trips to Costa Rica. There's no room in this school for a boy who had to learn to walk, talk, and eat solid foods twice in his short lifetime.

It's like Mason's peers are on an express train, and I'm chasing it with my now six-foot-two-inch son slung over my shoulder. The meeting with Charles was my attempt to throw him on board. Instead, I've landed with my face in the dust. Mason might look different. So do I. I saw it in Charles's face—pity and a little fear. It scares me too.

After dinner Alan and I talk.

"I wish I'd gone with you," he says.

"There's nothing you could've done differently," I answer defensively.

"It's not that," he says. "It was obviously really hard on you."

I blink back tears and push away what all this might mean. "I think the only thing we can do is homeschool him."

I don't envy Charles for having to be the one to tell me we won't be catching up to the train, not now. It was a tough role, maybe an impossible one. And even though I didn't want to hear it, he had a point. Mason still struggles with finding the right words. His right hip doesn't move so well, which gives him an unsteady limp. He has a hard time getting around although he's walking without a cane and hardly ever falls.

"I'll make it work," I say. So what if I don't have that eight-to-three daily time slot for doing everything required to keep this family running? What could be more important?

We open The Mason School located at our kitchen table, where we lay out his textbooks and a laptop. We enroll Mason in an independent study program, which gets us a weekly meeting with Mrs. Zwerin, a skilled and supportive public school teacher, who loads him up with assignments to keep him on pace with the ninth-grade curriculum.

I believe that Mason will go to college and get a job. I believe he will have girlfriends and maybe a wife. He will have a life. There's a lot of ground to cover between here and there. We continue his twice-weekly speech therapy and physical therapy at the gym. We hire an educational therapist to build Mason's reading and writing skills and an algebra teacher to make sure he stays on course.

Team Mason is a great group—and they get his jokes.

<br>

*thirty-one*

# Urban Legends

The only thing harder than parenting a child through a tumor and a traumatic brain injury while sustaining a marriage, I imagine, is doing the same thing as a single parent. I need Alan. He needs me. And frequently we drive each other crazy.

We return to couples counseling as we've done over the years whenever one or both of us need tools we didn't get from our divorced parents before they were older, wiser, and recoupled.

Our new counselor is named Dan. I like him because he's able to translate what I'm saying into language Alan understands. Dan is thin with white hair to his shoulders. He'd look like a Zen priest if it weren't for his penchant for leather biker vests and his liberal use of a certain expletive that begins with an "f"—as adjective, verb, and adverb. He was recommended by two sets of friends, one of whom is still married.

"It would be easy to get lost in the story of Mason's tumor," Dan says, "but what's real between the two of you right now? You're both doing amazing work for your family. But are you bringing your most depleted, empty selves to the relationship?"

*Uh, yeah.*

Today we present Dan with a non-life-and-death problem. Alan's father is insisting that Alan go on a trip to rural Canada to photograph eagles with him.

"Because of me, Alan can do whatever he wants. He never has to worry about who's going to take care of the kids, Mason's therapy, his homeschooling . . ." My voice ascends an octave or two.

"You could come on the vacation too," Alan says.

I stare at him disbelievingly. "So you think that's a vacation for me? What about time for the two of us?"

"I never get to spend time with my dad. We see your parents all the time," Alan says.

"That's because they help us. Besides, you're gone all the time." I'm talking through my tears. "I'm always home by myself. It's so hard. I'm lonely."

"Someone has to pay the bills," Alan snaps back.

Dan's head bobs from Alan to me and back. "Can we hit the pause button right there? This situation is incredibly hard on both of you."

I attempt an inhale as Alan continues.

"I'm lonely too. All this travel isn't exactly fun. Nothing I do is ever good enough for you," Alan says. "You're never happy."

This is one of our old standards, a worn-out cassette tape re-released as an MP3.

"Just because I'm sad doesn't mean I'm accusing you of anything," I say.

Finally Dan intervenes with, "It f—ing never works when my wife and I go back and forth this way," he says. "Alan, your wife wants to spend time with you. She's lonely and overwhelmed. Janine, your husband wants to be appreciated. He's lonely and overwhelmed. You're both good people in f—ing awful circumstances."

Incredibly, we spend the next twenty minutes (and $175) arguing about who is entitled to feel lonelier and more overwhelmed. Dan tells us our time is up. I write him a check. We set up the next appointment.

I'm mad, but I don't want to go home and eat yesterday's stir-fry. "Do you still want to get dinner?" I ask Alan.

"Yeah," Alan answers. "We might as well take advantage of the time."

"Good." I sniffle. "I'm hungry."

We settle into comfortable leather seats at a steak house nearby. I pretend to read the menu, struggling to compose myself. One deep breath. Another.

"I'm f—ing sick of all of this," I say.

Alan laughs. I laugh. We hold hands, tentatively, like people who are just getting to know each other.

I lose the go-take-pictures-of-eagles argument. On New Year's Day, Alan drives to Vancouver. I hand him a grocery bag packed full of protein bars and nuts, a grudging but loving offering.

"Thank you. I'll bring you some great photos." He kisses me.

I have a friend who says, "Would you rather be right or happy?" The implication being that any sane person would choose happy. But being right makes me happy. It's also my most dangerous state because my thinking is all knives and tallies.

Joan answers on the second ring.

"How are you doing?" she asks.

"Alan's in Canada with his dad," I say. "Sarah's got a new tutor. Austin's signed up for college classes this fall. I'm looking into a new form of therapy for Mason. It's called functional neurology."

"No. I mean *you*," Joan asks again.

"Me?" I want to laugh, a bitter, witchy cackle. Instead, I consider her question. "I'm mad at Alan. He wants me to go on vacation with him. As if I can just take off and have *fun*."

*Fun*? That word again. I hate it. I'm depleted to the marrow of me. All I want is to crawl into bed and watch TV.

I'm grateful when Sarah brings home the flu. No driving, no appointments, no guilt. We have to stay home; it's the responsible thing to do as virus-y people. So I stay in bed and watch old movies with my daughter.

This is how it is. This is what fun looks like. Instead of judging myself for my fun ineptitude, I sip my tea and pull the blankets around us a little tighter.

After homeschooling Mason halfway through his sophomore year, we find an alternative school where classes are taught one-on-one. The school is full of kids with all kinds of challenges. Some have ADHD. Others have physical illnesses. Some just don't like the typical high school scene.

I meet with Madeline, the enthusiastic head of the school. "Mason's speech is still affected by the hemorrhage," I explain. "But he's a smart guy, doing really well in school. His short-term memory is a challenge, but we expect it to keep getting better."

I'm embarrassed by the pleading desperation in my voice. It's hard to be so visibly needy, but homeschooling is difficult. Mason is eager to be around kids his own age.

After a tour of the campus, Madeline asks Mason, "What do you think?"

I telepathically nudge him to stand a little straighter and speak clearly.

"Stu-pen-dous-ly"—he pauses—"awesome."

The school agrees to take Mason, and I feel physical relief. My spine lets go as if I've ceased to be at war with gravity. They set up a structure so Mason's teachers reinforce his memory tools and speech therapy practices. I quash the worry that nothing could be this perfect.

When I pull up in front of school a few weeks later, Mason is frowning, a double-sided full-face downturn, which is its own kind of progress. He tosses his backpack in the back seat with a *harrumph*. I've been a mother long enough to know what comes next. He's frustrated, so it must be my fault. Lately the kids come at me with teenage attitude, slinging it at what feels like a cardboard cutout mom that's not actually me.

"I don't understand why I can't go out with the kids after school," he says. "Everyone went yesterday but me."

"You didn't ask," I say.

"I did too," Mason insists.

This is a memory-loss thing. The more I press, the more likely he is to dig in and create a version of what happened to fill in the blank space left by radiation.

"Where did they go?"

He looks at me, puffed up and angry. "I don't know," he says. "But I'm blaming you."

Mason says it like it is. I have to laugh. This time I don't take it on. But I'm trying to please everyone still, again and always, even though I've been told it's impossible. Alan might be making up for lost time at work. So am I. We hurry across town to Sarah's basketball game. I'm parsing myself out as best I can. I don't want to miss anything, especially this game. When Sarah's middle school hired a new PE teacher, he announced there would be a boys' basketball team. "Why not girls?" Sarah asked. The coach told her if she could recruit five other girls, they could have a team. She did. She's never played basketball, and neither have most of her recruits; what they lack in skill they make up for in grit.

Before the first quarter is over, the ref is blowing his whistle, and my daughter is on the floor wrestling the ball out of the hands of her opponent. She wins possession. The opponent walks away with a grim look on her face while Sarah jumps up and high-fives a teammate. It's a good place to practice not pleasing everyone. Maybe there should be a league for mothers—then the children could yell how wonderful we are from the bleachers and bring *us* healthy snacks so we don't get cranky on the ride home.

———

Annie picks me up for a hike one morning when I feel like a failure as a mother and a person. I'm angry at Mason. This is like being mad at Bambi.

"What's going on?" Annie asks.

I rerun the past few weeks to decide how best to answer this big question.

"Mason lost his phone—again. I tracked it down in an Uber on Lombard Street. I paid the driver to bring it back. It was the third time in as many weeks," I explain, my pitch rising with the feelings I've been avoiding.

"Of course you're frustrated," she says. "How could you not be? It's all too hard. Nothing is going according to plan."

What's lost in my aggravation is the miracle that Mason is able to use his phone, take an Uber, and carry on a conversation with the driver. Six months ago, I would've been in awe. Now I have trouble tracking how far we've come. It's like we're in the middle of a lake, and I can't see shore in either direction.

"Is it really about the phone?"

Of course it's not. Mason's educational therapist quit unexpectedly because I couldn't force Mason to keep a routine. And it's my fault. I am supposed to make Mason charge his phone and computer, have the right books ready, and be dressed, which means not getting sidelined with a thirty-minute shower or sketching at his desk when he's supposed to be eating breakfast.

A more together mother would have him shined and polished, waiting at the table for their session. The problem is that I'm not supposed to shine and polish him myself. It's easy for me to plug in his phone, gather the books, and lay out an outfit for a foggy morning. But I can't make him do it on his own.

I've tried being sweet, kind, and understanding, saying, "Now's a good time to charge your phone. This is a great habit to get into before you go to bed." I've tried bribery. "We'll get ice cream if you check all the boxes on your whiteboard three days in a row." I've tried being firm. "Do it. You have to do this, every day!" Or else, what? I'm not sure.

Still the phone blinks at me in the morning, 1 percent charged. The computer is somewhere in his backpack, which might have been left at school. He's wearing shorts, and it's 50 degrees outside.

"It's like I'm trying to force these connections in his brain," I tell Annie. "'Executive function' is what the therapist calls it, and he's worried that Mason won't get it back if he doesn't start doing these things now. He insists that if I set up the right system, Mason will follow through." I exhale. "It's not like boys this age are known for their organizational skills. Then pile a brain injury on top of that. I bought four different kinds of dry-erase boards; that made *me* feel better for about fifteen minutes."

"This therapist doesn't live with Mason, does he?" Annie asks.

"You're not supposed to feel this angry with your brain-injured kid. It's wrong, maybe pathological. I'm a horrible person. I'm responsible for so much but have power over so little."

We step aside to let an elderly man with three dogs pass us on the trail.

"What would you say to me if I was feeling that way?" she asks.

Baffled, I answer, "I have no idea." I'd never call my friend the names I call myself or question her character.

"You'd tell me that you've felt that way before, too, that you understood."

"Oh, right."

Everyone I know has stuff, and stuff is hard. Contrary to urban legend, there are no perfect parents or perfect kids.

I'm downtown picking up new basketball shorts for Sarah when I bump into Elinore, who used to be our neighbor and my good friend. Way back when, we spent hours at the park together while our sons swung from the monkey bars.

"How's everyone?" she asks.

"Good. Austin just started college in LA. Sarah's in eighth grade." I run through the stats. "And Mason's at a great high school, doing well."

"Oh my God, what you've been through."

I nod and ask, "How's Luke?"

I notice now that the skin is loose around her eyes and the roots of her normally well-maintained blonde hair are showing. Her eyelids are red-rimmed.

"Luke's in Marin General. He had a breakdown two nights ago. He's been shooting cocaine."

"Oh, El." For once, I'm the one who doesn't know what to say or how to say it.

"It's been so awful," she says. "But then I think of you and how lucky we are. I just don't know how you do it." She blows her nose into a shredded tissue.

I don't say, "I was just about to say the same thing to you."

It's hard to be the mom of a kid with a tumor in his head. But is it worse than having a son who shoots cocaine? It's likely a human quality that causes us to measure our misery by the yardstick of other peoples' tragedies, leveraging a secondhand gratitude, which is better than no gratitude.

Before saying goodbye, Elinore and I hug. She doesn't let go right away, and neither do I. There are no words. This might be the point, two scared mothers holding on to each other a little longer, not alone in this moment. The rest of the day I wear Elinore's mascara smeared on the shoulder of my gray sweatshirt.

# Bread

I spend time with an old friend whose child is dying of the kind of brain tumor Mason was lucky not to get. I felt myself a little bit above my head, floating. I didn't know what to say besides this is wrong, terrible, and hard. So I didn't say much. I sat with her. I held her hand and cried alongside her.

Mason is better but not *all* better, not yet. Five years have passed since we returned from Houston. The radiation appears to be working. Mason no longer has headaches on a regular basis. The MRIs show the tumor not doing much of anything, so we have longer breaks between anxiety-provoking scans. We are fortunate people, "blessed" with a "good" tumor. And Mason still struggles every day.

Me too. Some days I feel more defeated than others. I wonder, would it be so hard for God to give me a vision? A small star, a flash of light, Mary standing outside my bedroom door? But the answer to all questions seems to be "not right now."

I tell myself it's a process. It's just taking more days, more weeks, more months, more years than I imagined it would. I put my arms around my tall, somewhat wobbly son. He wraps his arms around me, his left side cooperating; the right delayed. He's tired all the time too.

"I really believe that we wouldn't be the family we are if I hadn't had this cancer," Mason says as we're driving to the gym one Tuesday.

"In what way?" I ask.

"I'm much closer to you and Dad," he says. "We get to spend a lot of time together. That's remarkably special. Don't get me wrong, I'd much rather have not gotten cancer."

Our laughter is a defiant prayer.

My brother, Tom, calls to see how we're doing. He doesn't call to tell me his daughter has been accepted to college, but he tells me that too. After we hang up, I lie down on my bed and cry. I'm happy for my niece, of course. But Mason was born one week before she was. Mason is not going to college next year. The distance between Mason and his peers is gaping and obvious now.

"He's alive," Alan reminds me. I am grateful. Really.

My child survived due to miraculous, science fiction–like interventions. We're thankful that the physical world for now, though not conquered, is subdued. But it's the spiritual world that's perplexing. I need to believe there's a path and purpose (beyond Mason living in a dorm next year). Even with my extra-thick corrective lenses, I can't get a clear picture.

I believe that God's got this. I'm about 72 percent sure.

---

Mason has been getting back and forth to school and to his appointments on his own for a couple of months now. It works as long as I guide him via cell phone every step of the way. He hardly ever loses his phone anymore.

Today I have a meeting at Sarah's school, where there's no cell reception. I set a reminder for Mason's afternoon appointment in his phone, write it on the refrigerator whiteboard, and remind him twice over breakfast. When I'm ready to leave, I ask him where he's going today.

He looks at me blankly, a little panicked.

"School?" he asks.

"Today's Friday," I say with all the patience I can muster. "There's no school on Fridays. What do you do at two o'clock every Friday afternoon?"

"Acupuncture?" Mason guesses.

"PT," I say. "With Brian."

He's had the same physical therapy schedule for two years now.

"Okay," he answers.

My anxiety rises around one thirty, and I repeatedly check my cell phone as if I can pull in the cell signal with the power of my worried mind.

At one forty-five, I finally borrow a landline and call Mason.

"Are you on your way to PT?" I ask.

"No, I'm at school." I hear the anger and frustration in his voice. "There's nobody here."

I can never be out of cell range, ever again.

When he finds me in tears, Alan says, "It's part of the learning curve." I'm inconsolable, lost in that hopeless place: it's always going to be this way.

Wise friends taught me to seek out people with shared experience when I need help—people who get it without a lot of words. It's a connection that bypasses the head and lands deep in the core, a sense of being understood. I can feel so lonely in our not-exactly-normal circumstances. It would be easy to let the alone feelings pull me to the edge of the herd where the wolves and the wine in the box live. But I'm saved by people who share their stories like bread.

"I put on my lashes every morning and I go," my friend Vanessa says.

She's come out of remission with a virulent breast cancer. Her hair is short and platinum, and her lashes are long and perfectly adhered. I called her because she has experience living with loss and unpredictability, and she's still cheerful when she answers the phone, and not above using a well-placed expletive when necessary.

"I try to make a difference that I live today by helping one person, even if I just let someone in front of me in traffic," Vanessa explains. "It matters."

We'd both been told many times, "I don't know how you do it."

"Like we have a choice?" Vanessa laughs, as a person can when she's made a full body-mind-spirit surrender to whatever comes next.

---

I tend to hear others' experiences much easier than their opinions, which I can reflexively dismiss if they aren't in alignment with my own. I envision a firepit around which we gather, more tribe than herd now. This is the warm place where stories are told, and we share the deepest truth of how we're alike, undistracted by the details of our differences.

Vanessa gets me. And I've found that the only thing better than "being got" by someone who understands is being able to give this understanding away. There's an alchemy that transforms even the suckiest, most awful, shouldn't-be-happening experience when it can help someone else.

Friends introduce me to Lindsey, whose seven-year-old son has been diagnosed with a brain tumor. Oddly, his name is Mason too; he also loves to laugh, and he has the same kind of low-grade destructive tumor. It's a strange confluence of circumstance that results in an instant connection. We've been talking by phone for months now. The first time she called, I made a conscious effort not to scare her.

"Our experience is unique," I said. "A big bleed isn't typical." I tried to give her what I needed, which was a listening ear, no advice, no judgment, no hijacking the hardship, just steadfast acceptance. I shared my experience, and then I stopped talking.

Lindsey planned to drive to Los Angeles from her home in Seattle, spending a day with us en route. When she gets here, we hug hello. Little Mason wears wire-rimmed glasses. His hair is dark and still short since it was shaved for two different surgeries in as many months. His sister, Greta, has silky blonde hair and clear eyes that tell you she doesn't miss much.

"Do you want to feel my horns?" little Mason asks. These are the raised spots under his scalp where his two newly implanted shunts live.

"Sure," answers my Mason, who now has the prefix "Big" before his name. Then Big Mason leans down so that Little Mason can check out his horns, which are now buried under thick hair. Little Mason lifts his shirt to reveal the new scar where the shunts drain into his abdomen.

"Check this out," Big Mason says, lifting his Giants T-shirt. There are two shunt scars, along with a puncture from the G-tube and a dash of scar just above his left breast where the port was inserted for chemo way back when. "I'm working on my six-pack," he jokes, and pats his belly.

"Well, you've already got a six-pack of scars," Sarah quips, not unkindly.

Both Masons begin to laugh. Greta joins in. It's the kind of laughter that builds like a tumbleweed.

Later in the kitchen, as I'm loading the dishwasher, Little Mason comes in.

"Can I ask you a question?" he asks. His mom is napping. His sister is hanging with Sarah.

"Sure," I answer, expecting something profound, deep. I'm a skilled mom, ready for anything.

"Why do you have so many cats?"

———

Somewhere I picked up the idea that a spiritually evolved person wouldn't feel like I do. She'd have answers, a better disposition, and probably weigh five pounds less. This one-day-at-a-time approach that I'm forced to live requires a level of presence and patience I'm not good at.

A few days after Little Mason's visit, Sarah comes down for breakfast while texting one of her friends.

Mason's eyes flare quickly, but he speaks slowly. "That's not fair. I want a phone."

"You got one for your birthday," I remind him.

His face lights up, like he's just opened the package.

It's like this with God and me. I feel hopeless. I feel afraid. My mind calculates risk and estimates what I can buy insurance for. A friend once joked that our minds are best suited for math problems. Meaning, data goes in and the synapses fire in search of answers. I can be so distracted by my mathematical abilities that I forget certain solutions are above my grade level.

"You don't have to know how any of this is going to work out," Joan says. "Remember you have a God in your life, and so do your kids."

This is where my short-term memory loss manifests as a spiritual malady. And I respond just like Mason. Palm to forehead. That's right! I'm in charge of very little. I survive on a messy grace that holds me upright and propels me forward from one day to the next. So far, there's always enough.

If it were up to me, I'd inherit a lifetime supply all at once and invest it wisely in something like a 401K. But it's more of a lunch-money situation.

*thirty-three*

# Expect

Alan turns fifty this year. I'm a young-ish forty-eight. We've been together nearly half of our lives, something I can barely wrap my head around even when I look at those early pictures of us with our unlined faces and brown hair. Alan's hair now has more salt than pepper. I've gone progressively "blonder."

The secret to our success may be that we haven't given up on each other on the same day. It helps that, so far, we've both been willing to change and grow, though usually not until we've exhausted blame as an option. But there's a tenderness evolving, and forgiveness appears to be a real possibility.

We were having dinner with some friends when someone asked how we made it through those six months in the hospital. Alan said, "It was the hardest thing I've ever done. I lost it more than once with a nurse or a doctor. Then I noticed that when Janine had a problem, she just dealt with it. She didn't even raise her voice. She taught me a lot."

I sat speechless.

"I didn't know you noticed," I said on the way home.

"Oh, I noticed." He smiled.

He also admitted he was wrong, but I don't rub that in. The point is that he can change. Apparently, so can I.

As the big birthday approaches, I offer, "Do you want to have a party?"

"That would be great," he says. "I heard an amazing band last week. I think they're pretty reasonable."

"What do you think, twenty-five or thirty people?" I ask, as if I haven't learned anything in the past quarter-century.

"You only turn fifty once," he says. This becomes Alan's mantra.

I hire a Grateful Dead tribute band to play in our yard, and I send an invitation to a hundred of his nearest, dearest friends. Then I hire a handyman who makes sure that the aged picnic benches don't collapse under the weight of it all.

I married someone who's much more outgoing than I am. I have a limited tolerance for exchanging the surface details of life with people I will rarely, if ever, see again. My husband, on the other hand, turns a few words shared with an interesting acquaintance into a friendship. So there are many people at the party I'm happy to see, many I don't know, and some I didn't need to see again. It's like a Facebook page, only real life.

Martina is one of the latter, a friend of an old friend, who's trying to catch my attention with an expression I recognize and recoil from, a pitiful contortion of the mouth coupled with sad puppy eyes.

"I think about you all the time," Martina says, clutching me by the shoulders. "I followed Alan's posts online. You poor thing. What you've been through." She releases me to touch her heart with both hands, her eyes pooling with real tears.

I want to run. Pity reflects how much my life really does suck. That I am different from other people in this uniquely awful life. There's a primal aversion to being singled out, an allusion to being outside the safety of the tribe. I don't want to be a victim of this tumor.

I don't want Mason to be. I don't want to orbit around it like a moon, but we do, still, and maybe always. Then again, we're standing under redwood trees in my very own backyard, surrounded by friends, and there's ice cream for dessert, which is the exact opposite of sucks.

A few yards away Mason laughs with my dad. Mason still has that expression, the eyes too young for the face, the right side drooping when he's tired. I can see that he's enjoying the party, the love he's getting from the many friends who are happy to see him doing so well.

"Are you okay?" Martina continues, grabbing both my hands to pull my attention back to her.

"Fine," I say. "Busy."

Sometimes I appreciate others' acknowledgement of how hard it's been. There are no medals for this work, no master's degrees or PhDs. But if I cried every time the subject came up, I'd wear out my corneas. People like Martina watch *Dr. Phil*, so they know that denial is bad, and airing emotions is good. She expects me to process with her. It's an intimacy I don't welcome, like a stranger's hot breath in my face.

"I'm so happy to see Mason." Martina dabs her nose. "How's he doing? Is the tumor in remission? Is this something he'll get better from?"

"He's doing well," I say, finally having learned not to pull out detailed medical records or my deepest fears at parties.

"Planning this party must've been a good distraction for you," Martina says.

"I don't need a distraction. My life is great."

As Martina looks at me disbelievingly with those big, sad eyes, I realize that what I just said is actually true. Yes, the opposite is also true. Many days we root for midnight and hope memory loss will erase indignities best forgotten. But he's still here. In this moment under the trees, Mason dances, long-legged, gravity defying, and fabulously uninhibited. He sings loudly, and so does Alan, who also hops high, pumping his fist in the air.

I excuse myself from Martina, pulled by the unstoppable urge to dance with my guys.

My life: it's a little bit of this, a little bit of that.

———

I'm sure everyone is overreacting. That includes the nurse practitioner who booked this urgent appointment. It's got to be more "atypia," which I'd been diagnosed with a few years ago—not cancer, but not quite normal either. Just a spot on a mammogram, a minor uncertainty heaped on top of the haystack that I try to protect from open flames. Annoying but not a crisis.

"I'm concerned that this has come on so suddenly," the surgeon says. "I'd like to biopsy it right away."

"Whatever it is, it can't be life threatening," I insist.

"No," he says.

"It's not going to kill me?"

"No," he repeats. His voice is kind, matter-of-fact. "If it's anything, it's DCIS."

Ductal carcinoma in situ (DCIS) means abnormal cells in the milk duct. It's considered stage zero breast cancer, noninvasive, until it's not.

———

My biopsy incision is deep. I can't drive for five days. My mom comes to take care of us while Alan works. She drives the kids to school and feeds us well. Alan left for Washington, DC, on Thursday morning.

"Are you sure you're okay? I can cancel this trip," he asked.

"Don't do that. I'm used to the waiting. My mom can handle everything."

All I want is to be left alone to catch up on all those episodes of

*The Good Wife* I've been hoarding on the DVR. I can't have breast cancer. I have a son with a brain tumor. This family has already ticked the cancer box. Besides, I'm the caregiver, not the care-receiver.

I am oddly okay. There's a blank space between me and "what could happen," where I imagine God bides His time. My grandma had a plaque with the Serenity Prayer: "God, grant me the serenity to accept the things I cannot change; the courage to change the things I can; and the wisdom to know the difference."

I recognized this prayer when I started to hang around sober people. I say it now because I want God to hear my voice and remember my lifelong deferment from anything that requires hospitalization, much less MRIs. But the words come out wrong. I say, "God, grant me the serenity to *expect* the things I cannot change . . ."

I hope this isn't an omen.

For dinner, Mom makes meatloaf with roasted yams and green beans. By seven p.m. the kitchen is spotless. Mason and Sarah are downstairs watching television. When the phone rings, I assume it's Alan, but it's Dr. Goodson.

"I'm sorry to call you at home like this," he says. "But your pathology came back. You have DCIS. The results took me by surprise," he adds. "It's considered stage zero cancer. This is something that can be treated. I want to get you in here right away so we can go through the options."

We set up an appointment.

"I'm sorry to call you like this," the doctor apologizes. But I'm glad he did. I'd rather get the news in my kitchen than in a medical building where I'd be forced to ride the elevator with strangers afterward.

"What is it?" Mom asks.

"DCIS," I say, not really believing it.

She begins to sob. "Why couldn't it be me? It should be me. I'm old."

I put my arms around her. I don't cry because the kids are

downstairs, and Mom is already crying. I'd rather be annoyed by her tears than feel the threat that is just beginning to filter through my consciousness. I think about how much I cried when Mason was diagnosed, how this scared Sarah, probably Austin and Mason too. I push that thought away.

I call Alan. I'm lost inside myself, far away from the feeling part of me. It's like I'm telling someone else's story.

"I'll be there as soon as I can." Alan's voice is hoarse. "I'm so sorry I left. I should be there with you right now."

I forgot that with biopsies bad news tends to come quickly. Good news doesn't because it must be double- and triple-checked before anyone with malpractice insurance is comfortable giving a pass.

"Jel, I love you," Alan says. "I'll be on the next flight home."

"I love you too," I say. "Dr. Goodson says even if it is DCIS, it's not going to kill me."

These are the right words, the truth. They have to be.

———

"The good news is, there's no evidence of invasive cancer," Dr. Goodson tells Alan and me. "The bad news is, high-grade DCIS is more likely to break through the walls of the milk ducts and spread into the breast, becoming invasive cancer. Because of the location, the size of your breast, and the high grade of DCIS, I'm recommending mastectomy."

I don't cry. I tuck away tears and terror where my breath belongs.

When we get home, we gather the kids and share the news. Austin is home for the weekend.

"It's actually not awful—something that can be surgically removed. I'm not going to die from this," I say. Then I think of what our lives would be like if Mason's cancer could have been cut away, how easy that would've been to be done with it quickly and decisively.

Sarah cringes reflexively. Austin and Alan tear up. Austin puts an arm around me, and I wipe away a tear that's slipped past lockdown.

"I'll sit with you in the hospital," Mason says, forming each word with care.

"Thanks," I say.

I reassure Annie (and myself) that I'm attempting a Jedi mind: not falling off the emotional or mental cliff. I detach from this body, careful not to breathe too deeply into that feeling part of me from the neck down. This was my instinct as a five-year-old girl preyed on and afraid. Up and out of this body was my only defense when I couldn't run or hide. It's a reflex I don't mind in this moment. I hover somewhere near the ceiling, a safe distance from the hurt and fear. I'm numb.

I organize the kitchen junk drawer, throwing away pencil nubs, dried-up pens, and keys to unknown doors. In the bathroom I go through drawer after drawer, tossing blushes that were never my color and used-up toothbrushes. When I don't know what to do with myself, I return to these rooms and feel the triumph of order that is only possible in a drawer.

That Sunday, Annie and I drive to church. Her grandson is in the back seat, whirling a Lego hero in the air.

"Do you want to ask for prayer today?" she asks.

"I haven't told many people what's going on," I answer. "I hate to use the *C* word when the doctors don't think I'll need radiation or chemo. It doesn't seem fair to the women who have *real* cancer to call this the same thing."

"It's like training-wheels cancer," Annie jokes.

I laugh, but I recoil from that word. I just want this breast off me.

"DCIS isn't even considered cancer in Canada," I say. "If I moved to Montreal, I wouldn't have cancer at all."

I'm not sure it's even true, but I read it online.

"You're not moving, are you?" Annie asks.

"Not anytime soon," I say, wishing I could.

But there's no outrunning this. I envision a giant melon baller going after these rogue cells. What's defined me—this female body—won't ever be the same again.

*thirty-four*

# One-and-a-Half-Pound Prayer

I am not going to die—not today, probably not tomorrow. This is my mantra, plus *this can't be happening; make it stop.* It's like someone has cut the brake lines on the family minivan. My children's survival seems inextricably linked to my own. What's scariest about the cancer in my body is the threat to them.

I consider not doing breast reconstruction. But I think about Sarah and how traumatic a constant reminder of my vulnerability would be for her. Then I think of what it would be like to look at myself in the mirror with one breast. I don't like that either.

I decide to have "the flap procedure." The plastic surgeon will take fat tissue from my belly and transplant it into my chest. The upside is that I have a week before surgery to load up on pie. "Got to give the surgeon plenty to work with," I say, as Sarah and I laugh in the bakery aisle. That feels good. I throw some lemon bars in the cart too.

There will be MRIs of my right breast (the hopefully healthy one) every six months, and my doctor recommends Tamoxifen, which will decrease my chances of developing cancer in this breast; he details the side effects and risks. Nothing is without its downside.

That night I sit in bed scrolling through Facebook, trying to get my mind off cancer and dying. Before Mason's brain tumor I might have believed I'd be one of the lucky ones. Now I know I'm just as qualified as anyone else to be one of the two women in a thousand who dies of DCIS.

I reach under my T-shirt and cup the modest handful of my right breast. Then I google "What does an AA-cup breast weigh?" The answer is 1.5 pounds. Am I willing to live the rest of my life in the high-risk category, just to keep this pound and a half of flesh? Or should I opt for a double mastectomy?

When Alan comes home that night, I tell him, "I want to do both breasts. That way I'm done with this. I can't do MRIs every six months, and the inevitable biopsies. I can't live like that."

Alan is quiet. "I get it," he says.

I feel relieved. I need to get off this road, the sooner the better.

——————

I tell Dr. Goodson I want both breasts removed. He reiterates the studies, the low risk for the right breast, the safety of Tamoxifen. He explains that even if I did get cancer in the right breast, I would be monitored so it could be addressed before it became life threatening. He doesn't dwell on the fact that any cancer that has already escaped the breast will have its way anyhow.

"But I'll always be considered high-risk, right?" I ask.

Dr. Goodson nods. "If you do a double mastectomy, your risk isn't zero, but—for you—it goes down from 30 percent to about 3 percent."

I like those odds.

"I have to go for an MRI with my son every six months. I can't go for me too. I know what it's like," I explain. "Waiting. Not knowing.

Then there's the suspicious whirls on the scan. The 'it might be some-thing' biopsies. I've had two of those already. I can't live like this."

Panic rises at the thought. Would we schedule Mason's MRI and mine into one awful month or spread them out and stain the entire calendar with fear and mortal danger?

I know what it means to not die from cancer—to have to live with it.

I feel strong and clear about my decision. Then I read an op-ed by a writer I admire. She posits that double mastectomy is an ill-advised trend, like low-waisted jeans, and women like me are too hysterical to know better. She explains that the procedure doesn't improve overall survival rates. There's no mention of the psychological toll. No con-sideration that women like me might possess the reasoning ability and emotional intelligence to know what's best in the context of our own lives.

I've never read a similar warning about ignorant, scared men lop-ping off their man parts unnecessarily. We assume their due diligence. But women? The anger feels compelling, almost good, like the metal-lic taste of blood from a split lip. Alive.

Once my hands stop shaking and I put the newspaper down, I realize that the most radical act is to be true to myself. There's a still, strong voice inside me, and I know what's right—for me, just me. I don't know what anyone else should do. I'm so tired of being judged that maybe, just maybe, I'm willing to ask God to help me stop judg-ing others.

I'm in the hospital for two nights. We're lucky to have good insur-ance that pays for it. And I feel such relief being cared for.

On the first night a nurse close to my age comes into my room with a hairbrush and a ponytail holder. She sits on the side of my bed and gently untangles my hair. She doesn't rush, though surely she has other things to do. When she finishes, she makes a neat ponytail on the top of my head.

The next day, Dr. Goodson stops by. "Your lymph node is clear," he says. "So chances are you won't need chemo or radiation."

"Thank God," Alan says.

I try to take a deep breath, but it hurts too much. I don't look at my body until five-days post-op when I take my first shower. Scabby trails circle each breast. Across my abdomen, hip-to-hip, a ruffled red line marks the deep incision where they took my belly fat for the transplant. My eyes fill with tears. *This is the good news*, I tell myself. *I had something that could be cut off, and it's gone now.*

But I didn't have any scars before, not on the outside. Now my torso is a map of angry red lines. After the shower I sit on the bed, depleted, while my mom helps me maneuver into a tank top.

"How're you doing?" she asks.

"It's just a lot to take in," I say, motioning across my chest. "So nasty looking."

"Well," she says, "maybe you should look in the mirror right now."

I push myself up to standing, which requires awkward redirection to avoid engaging my abs and the long incision. Standing in front of the mirror, I laugh out loud.

My "I carried three babies," pouch-y stomach is flat, in sharp contrast with my perfectly shaped new C-cup breasts.

"Wow," I say. What a strange outcome. For the first time in my life, I look hot in a tank top.

I lay down for a nap and attempt to push away the grief, anger, and fear, but it's hard to do. Maybe it's got something to do with these deep wounds and the fissures in what I thought I knew for sure—that if I was smart enough, I could be safe. That safety could be found.

This powerlessness over my body brings back the other powerless times, slicing through a layer cake of hurts. Those times I was grabbed, groped, or worse. Believing it was my fault made me feel less exposed. If I could've done something to stop it, then I wasn't prey, and it might not happen again. One day I was a tiny girl whirling around in a pink dress, free and happy in lace-trimmed ankle socks. The next I was scared and hiding behind my mother's legs, with a secret too heavy for my forty-pound body. I'd dared to be too bright, too sure of myself. There was something wrong with me because the wrong person was drawn by a light I'd so carelessly put out into the world. This body possessed great power. It was both friend and deadly enemy, the house of vulnerability and hurt. I would deflect from what I thought was wrong with me, the shame I let define me deep down inside.

---

All those years I felt diminished, but what if I'm not diminishable?

Mason isn't less than he was before. Yes, I have to listen carefully when he speaks, especially when he's tired. I have to slow down beside him as he steps so gingerly, but it's a pace that lends itself to noticing. The essential Mason is more obvious. There's no swagger to disguise it, no sheen to deflect it.

As for me, I feared that something was stolen from me as a child, and my creed was to never let anyone know, especially the God who sorted people like dirty laundry into heaven, hell, or purgatory. But when I got sober and became acquainted with a God who was love and compassion (not judgment and criticism), a realization began to dawn. It's grown brighter over the years, and today it burns my eyes. No one can steal away the essential "who I am" that is worthy and whole. That God-spark isn't vulnerable to predators from the outside. What if that's true about the inside predators too? What if this cancer can't diminish me either?

It's too much to fathom, to take in. That familiar numbness filters through me, a cushion against the hurting body and overwhelmed spirit. But numb feels different today, familiar but not comfortable. If I can't feel pain, I can't feel much else either. The tears come, and I don't try to stop them. Not this time.

Joan comes over along with Annie and a few other friends. My kitchen fills with flowers and take-out. I forget to hurt. It's a short visit, all I can do right now.

I can't hug my friends goodbye. I can't even put my own mug in the dishwasher, bending is awkward and lifting impossible.

Joan takes the mug from me. "Let others take care of you for a change," she says, lingering after everyone else has left.

"I know but . . ."

"No 'but'! Go take a nap." She shakes her head.

When I wake up, she's gone, but the dishwasher is loaded, and laundry is folded.

Within a week I'm able to walk to the end of the block.

"I'll go with you," Mason offers. He takes slow, patient steps beside me. "So, Mom, are you a cancer survivor, too, now?" he asks.

"I guess so," I answer.

Technically I am. There's no such thing as a recreational mastectomy, but I feel like an imposter with my stage-zero situation and the new Victoria's Secret breasts—the ones I see but can't feel.

"We're cancer survivors together." Mason grins. He gives me a low high five since I can't raise my arm just yet. I force a smile.

I don't explain that it's easier for me to be a cancer survivor than the mother of one. That the scariest thing about me having cancer is the possibility of being taken away from the children who—I still believe—depend on me to keep them alive. One more time I'm reminded of how limited my ability to protect anyone really is. Also how ferocious my denial of this is, which tends to create a mental ping-pong game that has me chasing little white balls to the point of collapse.

I can't sidestep my way around this vulnerability. I can't tie pink satin bows and cheerful affirmations around my fear and anger. The point of not dying might be to feel these things, to have this human experience, including the infuriating part about being on a "need to know" basis with the universe. Would it be so hard to provide a script for next week? Even just two days from now? I'd probably have some great edits. I could be very helpful this way.

Mason taps the lamppost at the end of the block, then turns around on the sidewalk. I do the same. Each step takes effort and concentration in my rearranged, wounded body. I've been holding out, waiting for guarantees so I can stop gripping against threat and danger. I've convinced myself that someday (never today) I'll be able to relax because all my people will be fulfilled, happy, and well fed forever. But it seems there's very little in the destiny department that I'm actually in charge of.

As Mason and I make our way back home, it's clear my current job description is limited to left foot, right, inhale, exhale, repeat, then lunch.

Joan's advice: If you want real control, you have to let life have you. It does anyway.

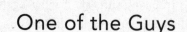

*thirty-five*

# One of the Guys

There's no way Mason is going to his high school prom. We didn't nurse Mason back to health only to have him slide off the deck of a party boat and drown in San Francisco Bay. I vaguely know this is my craziness talking, so I solicit a second opinion. I call the head teacher at his school.

"I'm concerned about the boat. You know how unsteady Mason can be," I say. "And he doesn't have a date."

It's hard to know which upsets me more: imagining Mason falling into the bay or Mason sitting alone in a corner while the other kids dance.

"I'll look after him," the teacher says. "We'll have a lot of adults there. I think he'll have a great time."

It's right to let him go. It's a triumph that he *can* go. Alan is all for it. So he goes.

The night of the prom, Alan helps Mason shave, then slicks his hair back with styling gel. Mason watches in the bathroom mirror while Alan buttons the top button of his shirt for him and laces a purple silk tie through his collar.

Mason points to the trach scar just above where the collar lands.

"The plastic surgeon could laser that scar away if you want," I say.

"Actually, I like it. I don't need tattoos. If I'm not tough, how did I get this many scars?"

We laugh. Mason pushes his weak right arm into his blue blazer, shrugging it over his shoulders.

I'm recovering from my surgery, driving again, though easily exhausted and still feeling vulnerable to elbows and airbags. I concede the transportation to Alan so I can stay home and focus my brainpower on worrying Mason into safety.

"You have your phone, right?" I ask.

Mason pats his blazer pocket.

"Have fun," I say in my most confident voice.

At seven p.m., when the boat is leaving the dock in San Francisco, I log in on Find My Friends and watch Mason float across the bay. The dot on the screen reassures me. If he did fall into the bay, I'm pretty sure the dot would disappear. I don't google the Coast Guard's emergency number just in case because that would be crazy.

At eleven thirty p.m., Find My Friends shows the dot on dry land, then traveling across the bridge and north on Highway 101.

Mason walks into the house grinning, blazer slung over his shoulder. Alan follows behind. He's grinning too.

"How was it?"

"It was amazing," Mason says. Then he trots up to his room, like the teenager he is, nothing divulged.

I give Alan a curious look.

"So I was waiting, watching the kids come off the boat," Alan reports. "No Mason. Then I see the last people exiting, and it's Mason and a woman. I think, *How sad. He's leaving with a teacher.* Only when they get closer, it's not a teacher. It's Amanda. A high school girl!"

When I pick up Mason from school on Tuesday, he meets me at the classroom door.

"I need you to sign a permission slip so I can go to Amanda's prom," he says, the words coming a little faster than usual.

Amanda goes to this alternative school for tutoring. She'll graduate from a nearby public high school, which is holding its prom in two weeks. Amanda appears with the permission slip. It's my job to make her like me, to be a helpful ambassador for my son.

"I can drive if that helps," I say.

"That's okay," Amanda says. "I can drive."

Of course she can. Girls Mason's age can drive. Boys too.

"Sounds good," I say, though I'm not exactly sure.

It's not hard to see my son as Amanda does—a boy who is kind, with strong features, beautiful eyes. He's tall and long-limbed, surprisingly insightful, goofy, and fun.

"You know how to be a good dancer?" Mason asks. "You don't care what anyone thinks."

I love this about him; it also scares me. Most teenagers can mask their vulnerability easier.

I don't want anyone to be mean to Mason, ever. He's always been one of the friendliest people I know. This didn't change when his brain was injured. Mason doesn't judge people. He's happy to get to know them and gives them room to be who they are.

Mason asks when he can drive. I want him to be able to. Really, I do. But last night after dinner, Mason sponged down the table while I finished loading the dishwasher. He asked, "What's for dinner?"

I looked up to see if he was joking, but he wasn't.

My heart didn't sink, my whole being collapsed inside myself. This might be the definition of despair: when I've let my guard down, relaxed into routine, even tentatively hopeful, and my son has no idea that he ate three tacos ten minutes ago.

"Well, you'll need to be able to remember where you're going," I answer, kindly I hope. He'll ask again in a few days; either the answer hasn't made that leap into long-term memory yet or he's hoping that it will change before it does.

For every missed milestone, my mind skips to my inability to plan how any of this can work out. I grew up worshiping brains; my family's greatest ability was to outsmart and outthink. This was how my parents got ahead. It's how my great-grandparents managed to propel the gene pool out of the Back of the Yards on the South Side of Chicago to the dorms at UCSD, where I ended up.

Survival came from figuring out a strategy and defending against threats. What does it mean that my son's life is not figure-out-able? That he's most vulnerable in this thinking part of himself?

Joan reminds me, "You can't possibly know what's going to happen next week, let alone twenty years from now. You'll know what to do when the time comes. Have faith in that."

I'm trying to believe that God is—as they say—Good Orderly Direction.

There was a time, not long ago, when the thought of Mason living to forty seemed impossible. Now the tumor is quiet. There is no indication that Mason is dying any faster than the rest of us.

When I look at Mason, I see his future split in two. One life looks the way it should have been (the way I planned it). The other life is how it's unfolding. Some might call this God's will, but I need God too much to attribute Mason's suffering to an advanced human spirituality course. And I'm starting to wonder how much I limit God by trying to understand rather than experience what is. What if God's will is fierce, unwavering love and strength no matter what the circumstances might be?

I google "recovery from brain injury" for the millionth time to see if there's a vitamin or a superfood I missed. I read, again, that most recovery happens in the first eighteen months post-injury. We're in year six, and there has been progress. Mason can walk, talk, keep himself groomed and fed, create amazing artwork, do geometry and physics, and clean the kitchen (when he feels like it). His teachers rave about how engaged and willing he is, how hard he works, how he doesn't complain or slack off. Yet memory loss makes reading, writing, and test taking difficult. The right side of his body doesn't always cooperate. He still has to work much harder than the rest of us to orient himself in this world from one moment to the next.

I am his PR representative when we go out in public. Just last week a waiter asked Mason, "How was your salad?"

"Hor-ri-fi-ing-ly . . ." Mason pauses.

The waiter looks panicked.

My mouth is open, poised to explain, but this time Mason finds his words before I do.

"Wonderful," Mason finishes with a flourish and a satisfied grin.

The waiter laughs, relieved. Sarah shakes her head. Alan and I, we laugh a little too long and smile a little too hard.

"So, Mace, what do you want for your birthday?" Alan asks.

"You're turning nineteen on the same day you graduate," I remind him.

His face transforms into a toothy smile. He still enjoys this benefit of short-term memory loss: good news is new, surprising, and wonderful each time it's repeated. That is until it makes the leap into Mason's long-term memory bank, where he can take it for granted, just like the rest of us.

"I don't know," Mason says.

Sarah is sixteen now, with definite skills. "Just go online, take a screen shot, and tell them what color and size you want," she explains. "I'll help you."

"Your sister has perfected the art of getting exactly what she wants," I joke.

"I would, too, if I wasn't so busy beating cancer," Mason says.

We heave a collective family sigh. We're used to this. It's a balancing act, not denying Mason's experience and not tethering him to it.

"I'd believe that if there wasn't an indent in the couch in the family room where you watch TV," Alan says, trying to keep the mood light.

"Excuse me," Mason pronounces the words clearly. "I can't hear you with that broccoli in your teeth."

Mason's comic timing has come through this experience unscathed. He attempts to lighten everything, from awkward social interactions to the unknown, looming future, with brightly colored strobe lights, ergo his goofy sense of humor. But he does get discouraged and lonely too. Being on a different road—in our case an unpaved goat path straight up a mountain of undetermined height—is by definition a solitary pursuit. I do my best to set up water stations along the way, seeking out friends who are not afraid to climb and sit in inclement weather.

I'm always looking for people with shared experience, who understand without a lot of words. Mason needs this, too, companions with muscle memory. So I'm thrilled to find a retreat for brain-injury survivors. Activities will be made safe for people with balance, memory, and other cognitive challenges, and trauma nurses volunteer as staff. Nothing could be more perfect. So we drive to the mountains, where Mason will spend a long weekend with teenagers like himself, rafting and exploring those off-the-grid trails together.

Coincidentally, the night before Mason's weekend retreat, Alan has a friend hosting a fundraiser nearby, so our first stop is a fancy house party where the theme is Neverland, as in *Peter Pan*. Adults wear fairy wings; some sport wands, others pirate swords. There are many lost boys and girls in feathers, boots, and animal ears. I'm dressed like Wendy, in a blue silk dress with a subtle grosgrain bow in my ponytail, a look I pulled together after too many hours googling Wendy options that wouldn't make me look like Bette Davis in *What Ever Happened to Baby Jane?* Mason hijacked Alan's costume as one of the Darling boys—a long, white nightshirt, top hat, and umbrella in case the opportunity to take flight arises.

One of the fairy women takes a liking to Mason. She is over six feet tall with thick silver braids and glitter tattoos on her forearms, sort of an Amazon fairy (mythical tribe, not online retailer). She finds us at various hors d'oeuvre stations and offers Mason cocktail napkins and affirmations.

"You look amazing," she says. "You are the brightest light here."

He smiles unfazed and eats another piece of balsamic-soaked watermelon.

We are seated later at a long table, waiting for our soup, when Mason excuses himself to find the bathroom.

Ten minutes later the Amazon fairy leads Mason back to our table.

"Look who I found," she says in a sing-song voice. "He was lost."

Mason shakes his head. It might've taken him a few minutes, but he would've found us.

"I was just telling Mason about a woman I know who designs trikes for people like him, people who are differently gifted, more abundantly gifted." She nods, clearly pleased with the sensitivity she's showing. "It's a wonderful thing."

She kneels between Alan and me.

"Do you want to come to the lake with us tomorrow? A friend has a house nearby. He is quite a healer."

"Oh, thanks," Alan says. "Tomorrow Mason is actually going on a retreat with a group of brain-injury survivors. It's something he's been looking forward to. It's been hard to find friends who have gone through the same thing."

Gold glitter falls into worried lines punctuating her forehead, giving her the look of an aging Klimt painting.

"I understand what you are going through. It's very important to turn this paradigm upside down. Using words like *injury* and *hard* only reinforce the negative. These children are so far ahead of the rest of us. They are not disabled. They are advantaged. I invite you to come up with some better language!"

Alan nods, looking a little lost.

She turns to Mason. "You are advantaged, Mason. You are better off than most of the rest of us."

Mason pauses, soup spoon midair.

"Please go away," he tells her.

Amazon fairy blinks back her surprise.

"Of course," she says, patting his shoulder, then mine.

"I understand," she whispers in my ear. "I don't take offense."

She flits off to her soup, which is cooling on the table behind us.

The gift of the Amazon fairy is that Mason remembers her two hours later when we're driving to the hotel. I cheer the new brain pathway.

"She was trying to relate," he explains thoughtfully, "which I find annoying because she has never been through any similar stuff. I like it when people care. But this idea that they know what it's like for me pisses me off."

No one wants to be walled off in a box of assumptions. Glitter won't change the fact that Mason's life is harder than his brother's, his sister's, or mine. Pretending it's not there doesn't take away pain. If anything, it takes away that essential "we" of the human experience that assures us we're not alone, wrong, or crazy.

I sigh. He's right, of course.

*Denial* is an unkind word, an accusation, but also a close personal friend. For all my emphasis on Mason's "good" tumor, "not that" chemo, and "better" radiation, there's no way to spruce up the word *catastrophic* when it describes the bleed in his brain. Same goes for my lightweight breast cancer. I can dress up in lace bras that they didn't make in my previous size, but alone in front of the mirror, scars trace the boundaries of what I can't feel anymore. Yet it could be worse.

I still have more questions than answers. Specifically, how do I sink into the experience and not drown in it? How do I stay honest without pouring pink paint on what's true? As always, my mind whirls. Then there's the eighteen-inch dive into the heart when we meet Mason's retreat roommate the next morning. Justin speaks slowly, like Mason often does.

"I work at a school." Justin chooses each word carefully. "I help with the second graders."

There's space between his words that we know not to fill. We lock our attention on this friendly boy with thick black hair.

"Sometimes I coach in PE too," Justin says. "Soccer, basketball . . ."

Mason waits his turn, and when he can't stand it anymore, he interjects, "I . . . ," then "We . . ."

But Justin continues on, "I've been here four times now . . ."

A counselor waves Justin over to help another camper with his gear.

Mason shakes his head and smiles. "Wow, that kid can go on and on."

So can he. Then again, so can I. It was good to see him listen with the same kind of patience he appreciates from others. Here, he's just one of the guys. People understand the depth of what he means when he says, "It is what it is."

*thirty-six*

# The Charm of Hummingbirds

High school graduation is looming, or joyfully approaching, depending on how sleep deprived I am. The next step appears to be community college. Mason and I wait in the lobby of Student Accessibility Services for his intake appointment.

"The counselor will meet with Mason first. You know, confidentiality rules. If Mason wants to, then he can invite you in," the receptionist explains.

"Of course," I say, using my most agreeable "I'm not a helicopter mother" voice. I want Mason to fit in, to find his place with the least amount of intervention. That said, I've prepared a detailed list of questions.

As promised, the counselor, who introduces herself as Shelly, takes Mason into her office.

I stay in the waiting area scanning PuppyFinder.com on my iPad. I see Mason talking with the counselor through the glass walls, and I wonder when a reasonable mother might interrupt? There is about a 10 percent chance he will remember to invite me in. But I'm the only mother in the waiting area, also in the bookstore, or even the parking lot. This awareness gives me pause.

Ten minutes in, not even rescued Great Dane/Great Pyrenees puppies can distract me. I walk over to the reception desk.

"I'm sorry, but I really need to be in there. He forgot to invite me in." I sound very helicopter-y, alarmist even.

"She'll take notes," the receptionist offers helpfully.

"But he'll forget why he's here. He's got short-term memory loss," I say. "It's the disability we're here about. I have a list of questions."

She dials the counselor and whispers something into the phone. Within minutes, I'm inside the office.

"I need to go to the bathroom," Mason says, pushing himself out of his chair. This is another problem that's emerged, ranking number two behind memory loss as the hardest thing Mason lives with. It's a misfire in the brain that tells him he has to go, immediately, like right now.

The counselor walks him to the hallway and points in the direction of the restroom. She returns to her desk and folds her hands. Her expression is soft. She waits for Mason to return, but I jump in, knowing it's going to be awhile.

"When we called, they mentioned signing up for placement tests. He's going to need a scribe and a reader. Also, is it possible to break up the test so he doesn't have to do it all at once?"

"Yes," Shelly explains. "He'll have to complete it within a two-week period though." We sit silently for another minute before she asks, "Do you think he's lost?"

"He has his phone with him," I say.

My phone is facing up in my purse, poised for the call. A minute later the receptionist leads Mason back into the room. He takes his seat, and we resume.

"What about note takers?" I ask.

"The professor will ask for a volunteer," Shelly explains.

"What about classes that transfer to other schools?" Mason asks. He is an enthusiastic student, serious about his future.

Shelley pulls up a website and shows him how to find the courses required for various universities.

"Excuse me," Mason interrupts. "Where's the bathroom?"

Shelley looks surprised but collects herself admirably. Like a scene from the movie *Groundhog Day*, she points Mason in the direction of the bathroom, one more time.

"This is going to be a problem with his professors," she says, concerned.

"Yeah, that's why we're here. He has a disability," I say matter-of-factly. "It's a result of the brain injury."

I cringe for Mason and for myself. While my life strategy has been to keep my weaknesses tucked underneath a capable exterior, and not draw unwanted attention to myself, my son doesn't have this advantage. Sometimes this panics me. I've resisted using the word *disability* because I'm worried it will have the permanence of a tattoo. Brains heal. He has eight more years until his brain is fully developed.

"I'll have to write his professors and let them know," she says.

"Yes," I agree, "I think so."

After our meeting Mason points me in the direction of the restrooms, the route sketched in his short-term memory. It's progress, the kind of forward motion that others might not notice.

―――

I've convinced myself that if I can get Mason to drink eight glasses of water a day, his memory will improve. It's a theory I can hang on to because I can't disprove it. Still, I'm sure God and Dr. Fisher would agree with me. The problem is that since the G-tube came out five years ago, I've lost the ability to pour the liquid into Mason's body.

I find his full, untouched water bottle in his backpack most days.

"Your brain is shriveling up from dehydration. You haven't had anything to drink since breakfast."

"That's not true," he says, shifting in his chair. I don't believe him.

"You're not moving until you drink this water!" I assume the stern voice my mother used when she made me clean my room.

It's my version of the children's book *If You Give a Moose a Muffin*. If I'm stricter, he will drink water; if he drinks water, his cognitive function will be better; if his cognitive function is better, he'll remember new material in school, he will graduate, he will hold down a job, which means he'll make his own way in the world, which means he'll be happy. And if Mason is happy, and Alan is happy, Austin is happy, and Sarah is happy—then I get to be happy. It's the perfect formula, except it doesn't work.

Today I saw myself. Mason saw me too. I was the one with the problem. The feelings cut through me, the words, too, shards out of my mouth.

"This affects me too! When you don't take care of yourself, we all suffer the consequences." My voice is stretched and high pitched.

My mouth is dry. I realize I haven't had anything to drink since lunch. I pour myself a glass of water. Luckily, I can't talk and drink at the same time.

My needs? I don't want anything to do with them because needy people are not only annoying, they are vulnerable. They're also not in control of themselves or the family members who should be grateful for all they've done for them. I've spent my life walled in by other people's dire situations. I've made strides taking care of myself, at least not hurting myself anymore, sleeping, eating, and asking for help. But there's still a systemic weakness that throws me off balance, like underdeveloped quadriceps.

My friend Tom says he didn't think he had feelings; he was just angry all the time. I might be a little miffed myself. I had a plan. It was a good plan. I've been a good sport and revised the plan (several times).

Now we're supposed to get the heroic, miraculous ending, the moral to the story—good always triumphs; good is always recognizable. But that's not what's happening.

It's just one more long day, another dinner that Mason forgets he's eaten, another place set at the table for Austin, who went away to college last August.

But Something keeps nudging me into the here and now where the people who love me wait for me to let my guard down. It's such a familiar posture, I've confused it with my bone structure. As a child, I created that shield, the layer of protection between me and the world. The illusion is that this keeps me safe, but all it does is hold in the hurt.

I'm becoming willing to set the shield at the door with my muddy sneakers.

"I miss you," I say to Alan over the phone.

Not "you've been gone too much; you've been negligent" because we're both navigating impossibilities. He's trying to keep a business (and our family) afloat financially. I struggle to keep everyone alive, including the cats, who insist on running out the door even when the coyotes howl.

"I'll be home at four. Let's go for a walk," he answers happily.

Curiously, there's no defensiveness when there's nothing to defend against. We make our usual loop through the neighborhood, the dog pulling us from one mailbox to the next.

"I heard about a women's retreat," I say. "I could use some time away."

"I'll make it work," he answers. "It's a great idea."

I knew Alan would say yes. He always does when it comes to trying something new, an adventure. I'm the one charged with figuring out how the suggested activity might cause dismemberment, bankruptcy, or death. But I'm learning that I can't protect myself from life and all its messy consequences.

So I brave Highway 5, enjoying seven hours in the car, listening to whatever music I choose.

The retreat house is up a winding road. I see nothing but sky, parched grass hillside, and the Pacific. It's beautiful. I'm greeted by a smiling woman in yoga pants who hands me a schedule and points me to a dot on the map, a cabin where I'll stay with seven other women. I talk myself through it like I'm a small child. *It's okay, honey. It's just two nights. If it's too weird, you can sleep in the car or leave.* Inside, I lay my sleeping bag on the last available bottom bunk.

I know maybe five out of the eighty women here. I thought this would be a relief, a break from the heavy lifting of being me. But others are welcomed with big hugs and enthusiasm. It's eighth grade all over again, where to sit in the cafeteria, other women knotted in happy conversations, obviously more loved than I feel right now.

I wonder why I thought this was a good idea.

After dinner I sneak outside to call Alan. Regrettably there's no reason to hurry home. I give him what I think is a hilarious blow by blow, how certain women inspire actual worship within the group. How the regulars save the best seats for the spiritual talks, which seems ironic to me. I can't quite name what I'm feeling; all I can identify is how annoying these people are, how I might log in to Hotels.com if cellular data works with this weak signal.

"Give it one night," he suggests.

I grudgingly agree because I don't want to drive off a cliff on the winding, now pitch-black road back to civilization. I stuff my earplugs deep into my ears and fall into an exhausted sleep of necessity despite the flimsy mattress. I'm surprised when dawn streams through the cabin walls. I pull on my jeans and a sweatshirt in the bathroom so I don't wake my bunkmates.

I follow a path past the retreat center toward a bluff. I stand at the edge of earth, air, and ocean. The sky is a happy blue, the ocean reflects a moodier color a few shades darker. Framing the vista, a willow tree blooms with spiky yellow flowers.

I sit on a well-positioned bench and breathe it in. In my first weeks sober, someone told me that willows are the strongest of any tree because they bend with the weather. I close my eyes to meditate a few minutes. When I open them again, the willow is filled with a hundred hummingbirds drinking from its bushy flowers. It's a charm of hummingbirds, a rare sight.

The hummingbirds hover, bodies shimmering, wings moving too fast to register, an iridescent blur. I'm okay, I realize. Then the thought comes, *I simply don't do uncomfortable feelings. I look around to see who's to blame.* It's an old habit. I drop my irritation at the retreat people like it's a stone in the grass. It's not them. It's me. I'm not angry. I'm afraid.

I remember learning that "I am afraid" translates to *J'ai peur* in French—"I have fear." I wonder what it would be like to just hold fear in my hands and not become it?

Love was surely the first emotion I ever felt with my beautiful and painfully young mom and dad. Fear came in a close second, and there's an electric quality to the feeling that I've mistaken for being awake and alert.

Right now I feel the cool stone of the bench through my jeans. My fists unclench in my lap. Beyond the willow and the hummingbirds, the horizon stretches over the Pacific. The salted breeze is cold and clean. I'll go inside soon and get a hot cup of coffee and some cereal maybe. Then I'll look for someone who is sitting by herself. She's probably somebody I'd like to know.

*thirty-seven*

# Just Dance

Today Mason will graduate from high school. After the official school ceremony, we'll celebrate with seventy-five or so of the people who have supported us—who sent care packages, delivered dinners, prayed, tutored, provided speech and physical therapy, along with companionship and compassion. They're Mason's teachers and therapists, our friends and family. Five years ago, when we wheeled Mason off the plane, he could speak only a few words. Everyone coming to the party knows what an achievement this graduation is, and they've helped to make it possible.

The school has rented a room at a Mill Valley hotel with a view of San Francisco Bay. Mason's grandparents fill an entire row of seats. Outside, rays of sunshine cut through the overcast morning; slices of silver shine on still water. Annie sits a few rows back. It's a small school, still getting started, so there are only six graduates but lots of supporters.

Mason is in the lobby with his classmates when "Pomp and Circumstance" begins. My eyes well up. The short parade of graduates enters in their purple robes, mortarboards, and silky tassels. Mason smiles wide as he passes us, one exuberant giraffe step, then another. He is gorgeous, those eyes, the sly grin. There's an asymmetry that gives away the difficulty. The way muscles grip the bones of his face, his eyes so pure and clean, unjaded by the certainty that some nineteen-year-olds have that destiny has put them in charge of a lot more than is actually possible. I don't notice that Mason's missing his tassel until Annie sneaks up the aisle and attaches one to the button on his mortarboard. We still need a lot of help most days.

I inhale this moment, the precipice of what's next. In the glow of this achievement, anything seems possible. I take another deep breath, which buoys me in the right now where, as Joan once told me, "God lives." In Hebrew, the word for *spirit* can be translated into "breath" or "wind." I don't hold my breath like I used to. Often I'm not afraid to inhale deeply, most days anyway.

I know less about God than I did before. But I believe more. It might have something to do with emptying out what I knew for certain, those boxes I tried to fit around Infinite Power to accommodate my finite human mind. I don't think God gave Mason a tumor or me breast cancer to teach us a lesson, though we've learned plenty. Same goes for alcoholism and knotty relationships.

I'm suspending my need to understand why because, as Dr. Fisher once said, "There are some things that can't be known." Trying to figure it out might always be my first reflex because "why" gives me the illusion that I can bend what-can't-be-happening into acceptable shapes with my mind. It's like kneading dough. But what about what's happening despite my best efforts? What I can't control? How do I live with that?

This new belief is tactile. It comes from having touched down into a source of strength bigger than me and strong enough for tidal waves of circumstance. I still have my list; I'm expected to do good and be kind, then left foot, right foot. It's not about the idea of God in my brain; it's about the experience of God in my life. Maybe "how" is a better question than "why" because we've been cared for, always and still. That's what I know.

The ceremony is personal. Each graduate is given the opportunity to say a few words. The five kids ahead of Mason decline to speak, but I know that Mason won't miss a chance at a microphone.

"I've had a pretty amusingly tough life," he says. "I had some problems starting out, and my teachers were awesome. Talk about committed. I just want to thank my teachers for moving metaphorical miles for me."

Tears roll down my face. Alan squeezes my hand. His eyes are filling too.

"He did it," Alan whispers to me, "and so did we."

And so did God. Grace showed up for us, through us, and sometimes despite us. I send up a silent *thank You.*

At home, the party is overwhelming—in a good way. I think of my grandfather releasing his belt a notch or two after a big dinner. That's how the gratitude feels inside me, full, pushing the limits I formerly thought were my own. I talk to too many people for too little time. I uncover another tray of chicken, toss more salad. Alan laughs loudly, as he is known to do. We hired a band composed of teachers from Sarah's high school who play classic rock. Mason dances with his friends, his teachers, and therapists.

"You must be so proud," my mother-in-law, Janice, yells over the music.

"Absolutely," I say. "Proud and grateful."

Alan motions for me to come dance with him. The band starts up one of my favorites: "Feelin' Alright?" by Traffic. There are no words, which is why I dance, remembering what Mason said before the prom: to be a good dancer, you can't care what anybody thinks.

The next morning I hear the rhythm of Mason's feet on the stairs, a slow one-two, his left leg compensating for the weaker right.

"You're up early," I say. His hair is sticking up on the sides. His eyelids are heavy. Just like any other high school graduate the morning after. "Did you get some rest?"

"Yep," he says, opening the fridge. He puts a carton of eggs on the counter, pulls a frying pan from the drawer.

*Miracle* was the most-used word yesterday as Mason danced for hours and joked with his guests. It's hard to deny as Mason prepares his breakfast. Sometimes I don't remember this. I'm like someone who lives six feet from the ocean and forgets to open the curtains.

He turns, catches me watching, and smiles.

"So do I have school today?" he asks.

Often I can hide my disappointment. Today it's obvious, as my expression melts into grief. It's like when Mason gets tired and his right cheek and corner of his mouth droop. My optimism goes slack despite the miracle, the party, the love, and seven hours of uninterrupted sleep.

"You graduated yesterday," I say.

His eyes go to the spent ribbons on the kitchen table, the stack of cards.

"We had a party yesterday," I remind him.

"I hate memory loss," he says. "Grandpa was here?"

"Yes, and both grandmas, Brian, and the ladies from church. You still have some cards to open."

"Cool." His face transforms quickly. "I'm going to eat first."

He cracks two eggs and wrestles some no-nitrate sausages out of their plastic wrapper, pushing the awkward right side of his body to cooperate.

"How'd you sleep?" he asks.

"Good," I say. "I was tired. It was a busy day."

"Thank you," he says. "You guys are the best."

His eyes are wide. There's no filter or protection. I love this about him, and it still terrifies me. He began volunteering at the food pantry at church a few months ago. I almost didn't leave when I dropped him off and a guy named Jesus introduced himself—not the Spanish pronunciation "hay-SOOS," but Jesus, as in Christ. He's not one of our regular churchgoers, but a capable friend and regular food pantry volunteer promised she would look after Mason. So I pushed through my cloud of worry, exited the building, then watched through the window until Jesus disappeared and Mason began stacking bags of yams on a table. Then I left. After that, I'm told, Jesus attempted to heal Mason with a "laying on of hands." And that's when one of the church ladies pulled Mason out from under Jesus' nicotine-stained fingers.

"How dare you assume there's something wrong with him!" she scolded. Then she sent Jesus away with a loaf of bread and some donated vegetables. Mason laughed about the experience, but it struck a chord with me. Sometimes truth leaks out like this.

This morning Mason chops leafy greens for his scramble. I sip my coffee.

Some say we humans are created in the image of God. It's one more thing I don't understand. People can behave horribly, and my own shortcomings regularly remind me of my not-god-ness. But I can't deny what I see looking at Mason. The unrestricted kindness and unfiltered love, strength, and humor. This very well could be the image of God, of loving no matter what, of pushing through what appears to be impossible, and being here right now with the people who need you the most.

It's all those angles, the so-called imperfections that catch and hold the light; it's what's left when life sculpts the flesh of who we thought we were. It's the heart-busting feeling that comes from doing whatever it takes, especially when we feel inadequate and not up for the job. This is where I see a Power bigger than the human mind; some might call it God. And it exists in this moment, right here in my kitchen.

This may be the one thing that I know for certain.

# Acknowledgments

I am fortunate to have people in my life who taught me how to love fiercely and show up for others when things are hard. I am deeply grateful to each and every one.

Mason encouraged me to share my experience of being his mom through this critical time. I've tried to preserve his privacy and that of my family. I live with remarkable people. Sarah and Austin, thank you for everything, beyond measure. Alan believed I could do this even on the days that I didn't. When I got stuck, he said, "Tell the truth."

Anne Lamott knew I would write this book before I did and supported me every step along the way. I'm blessed to have such a generous and true friend, who always has good snacks.

My mother, Camille Grabowski, has proofread my papers since I learned to print my name in the top right-hand corner. I am grateful for her keen eyes and loving heart. My father, Tom Urbaniak, continues to trudge alongside me and support my family unconditionally.

My agent, Heather Jackson, had the foresight to see what this book could be and the skill to help me get there. Thank you to my strong and skillful partners at W Publishing, including Paula Major and W's marketing team. Debbie Wickwire and Daisy Hutton have been unwavering in their support and a pleasure to work with. Meredith

Maran provided a practiced editorial eye in the critical role of first human to read this manuscript. Friends responded to my "Does this make sense?" e-mails: Barbara Rick, Tracie Morris, Rebecca Dolan, and Terri Tate. Natalie Goldberg has been a godsend to writers, and especially to me.

There would be no book if I hadn't survived these experiences and the process of writing about them. Thank you: my brother Tom Urbaniak, Janice Reid, Art Fluter, Cecelia Soboleski, Joan Reynolds, Cynthia Rangaves, Julie Childers, Jena Jensen, Michele Bousquet, Heather Huber, Lindsey Gordon, Rev. Veronica Goines, and William Goodson, MD.

I am forever grateful for the skill and kindness of Paul Fisher, MD; Patricia Murphy, ND; the neuro-oncology team, and everyone at Stanford's Lucile Packard Children's Hospital; Dr. Sergio Azzolino; also Dan Curry, MD, and the Texas Children's team. To all who have helped and prayed for Mason: thanks and love beyond words.

# About the Author

Janine Urbaniak Reid was born in Chicago and grew up in California. Before she began raising a family and then writing full-time, she was vice president of a San Francisco public relations firm.

Janine has been published in the *Washington Post*, *Chicago Tribune*, and *San Francisco Chronicle* and is widely syndicated. Hoping to bring humanity into the healthcare discussion by sharing her experience as a mother of a son with a brain tumor, she penned a piece for the *Post* that went viral. She has been interviewed on national news networks and continues her work as a spokeswoman for healthcare justice.

Janine writes about her imperfect life, what connects us, and addresses the question of what it means to love fiercely in a sometimes dangerous and always uncertain world.

Janine is a graduate of the University of California at San Diego and lives in Northern California with her family and a motley assortment of pets. She attends St. Andrew Presbyterian Church in Marin City: all are welcome.

For more information, please visit
JanineUrbaniakReid.com